# what do I
# ReAlly want?

# what do I ReAlly want?

## a guide to personal happiness

# LLOYD LALANDE

HarperCollins*Publishers New Zealand*

First published 1995
HarperCollins*Publishers (New Zealand) Limited*
P.O. Box 1, Auckland

Copyright © Lloyd Lalande 1995

ISBN 1 86950 180 2

Designed and typeset by Pages Literary Pursuits
Printed by HarperCollins, Hong Kong

*To Clare*

*This above all ~ to thine own self be true*

William Shakespeare, *Hamlet*, Act I, Scene iii

# Contents

# Introduction

*T*HE focus of this book, as its title implies, is on making a shift from living a life that isn't really "you" to living one that is.

It is very common to lead an existence governed by an elaborate structure of disempowering beliefs and limitations, usually the result of childhood conditioning. Yet it is in everyone's grasp to live according to one's own self-defined values and ideals — to lead a life that is an authentic expression of the individual.

What we really want, deep inside, can be uncovered and made a reality, and doing this is essential to happiness and fulfilment. This concept establishes the tone of the book.

The experience of happiness or fulfilment comes from knowing and understanding our true selves and what, in our hearts, we want in life. By expressing our true selves we develop an appreciation of our real worth and potential; most importantly, we gain self-respect.

In the pages that follow, I examine why it is so vitally important to define and live one's own life. I draw attention to specific blocks and disempowering influences, and provide effective guidelines for dealing with these. I establish the role of beliefs — and the behaviour these prompt — as the cause and determiner of one's life experience, and focus on clarifying the cause-and-effect relationship involved.

To live your own life as defined by you requires that you master new skills. I present techniques for defining what you really want, this being the bedrock of goal realisation. I also present the steps essential to identifying what you need to change and how to bring about that change, along with proven strategies that will ensure your new sense of growth and freedom continues to expand.

The content of this book is practical, and the ideas within it are applicable to all areas of life. It is offered as a guide both to those who are new to self-development and to those already some way along the path.

Lloyd Lalande
Christchurch, 1995

# Part I

# *Liberate your true self*

# 1

## *The greatest challenge you will ever face*

OUR choice of what we want in life is often influenced by our past. Childhood conditioning persists at the back of our mind. But it isn't only the past that influences our choices. The culture we live in also exerts pressure on our thinking and beliefs. This can cause us to go in directions which, in the absence of that pressure, we may not have chosen. What we think we want may not be what, in our hearts, we really want.

Some years ago I realised I had a choice: either I could continue to live in an automatic, unquestioning way, avoiding or denying my fears, or I could start living my life as an exploration — an exploration of who I was, what I believed and what I really wanted to achieve. The first choice was "safe"; the second confronted me with much that was unknown. If I had made a rational choice I would probably have played safe, but I was starting to realise the value of listening to my intuition. I chose the unknown. Although at the time I was unable to express myself in such terms, I wanted to find a life — a life of my own choosing, that excited me, stimulated me to learn, gave me a feeling of passion and added to my experience of aliveness. To this end I set about developing a degree of self-awareness, of accepting some aspects of myself and transforming others — a process that continues today. The aim of this book is to help you dismantle any disempowering influence that may be operating in your life so you can more freely walk a path of your own choosing, a path that enhances your experience of aliveness.

# Know and follow the real you

Inside each of us is a unique being waiting to express itself. We must ask ourselves what we want and look deep into our hearts for the answer. Where does your natural curiosity want to take you? What is it you would explore in this life?

*It is easy to live for others; everybody does. I call on you to live for yourselves*

Ralph Waldo Emerson

Ultimately you will not be satisfied until you are following the direction that the deepest part of yourself dictates. Your conditioned self might say, "I want a new Toyota, a million dollar house on the hill and a swimming pool." Your true self may yearn for a simpler life, saying, "I want a little cottage in the country where I can write, get to know myself, create a garden and hear the birds." You may be currently employed in an office or factory but deep inside secretly dream of having a successful business of your own. Perhaps you want to experience big business and be part of an exciting and fast-moving corporate world. You may dream of being an artist, singer, musician or writer. Or maybe you'd like to join with others to solve some of humanity's problems. Whatever it is that *you* truly desire, you can create.

Many of the personal development workshops and books available promote a "You can have it all, be the best, earn the most, be the richest, have the biggest, sell the most" kind of approach. Some even suggest the way to get what you want is to set such huge goals that the frustration of not achieving them will drive you to try all the more and hence ultimately make it. That's fine if it's what you really want, but *is* it what you really want? If you are learning to identify, nurture and follow your true self, you don't need frustration to motivate you; your natural drive to explore, express and expand will give you all the motivation you need.

Getting to know and learning to follow your inner self is

the greatest challenge you will ever face and offers the greatest joy and satisfaction you will ever experience. It can take enormous courage to stop and listen to your own inner voice and then act on its direction, yet high self-esteem and self-respect depend on it. You have everything it takes to make this bold move. You may find yourself going in a different direction from your family, your friends and what is considered normal, a direction for which there are no maps. You are unique, and when you express your true self you will be expressing that uniqueness. No-one can tell you what to do or how to do it. If you deny your true needs and desires, you will never feel fulfilled.

If your life isn't as you want it to be, something inside you must change. Your beliefs, expectations, goals, perceptions, feelings, fears and behaviour are the forces that shape your life. Whatever your current experience of life, if it isn't what you want it to be, disempowering conditioning is influencing you. The more self-aware you are, the more power you have to overcome that conditioning and create your ideals, making your life everything you *do* want it to be. In the words of humanistic psychologist Abraham Maslow, "Self-knowledge seems to be the major path of self-improvement." Without commitment to yourself, to peeling away the layers of conditioning that hide who you really are, your life will be one of unnecessary struggle, disappointment and dissatisfaction. Commit, therefore, to expressing your true self. Make your own choices. Let your uniqueness shine out — there is no-one like you on the entire planet. Give up trying to be like other people. Set about removing all the musts, shoulds, need tos and other conditioned thinking that limit your life to what it "ought" to be like.

Commit now, with unshakeable determination, to defining and manifesting your own vision and ideals. Dedicate yourself to what you want to be, do and have. Out of continuous commitment to what you are interested in, your passion will grow. It is loyalty to yourself that will remove any blocks that stand in the way of you materialising your dreams.

# But is this being realistic?

Is it realistic to think we can achieve our dreams? *Are* ideals achievable? Is it really possible to create an ideal experience of life? Can we create our ideal work and our ideal relationship? What about our ideal experience of ourselves — can we create that? You bet we can, and in Part IV of this book you will have the chance to define precisely what your ideals are and learn how to use feedback to make them a reality.

To create your ideals you must first believe it is possible to do so and then take appropriate action. Your beliefs shape your life, by creating your feelings and determining your actions. How you think and feel about the situations in which you find yourself determine what actions you take. If you know what you want and are prepared to change your strategy, you *can* create your ideals.

"Realistic" means "rooted in reality", or "based on facts". To decide, therefore, whether something is realistic or not, we must examine the relevant facts. What are some of these?

## *Fact 1*

### OUR BELIEFS ARE THE FOUNDATION OF OUR BEHAVIOUR

How we behave will always depend on what we believe, even when the cause-and-effect relationship is not at first apparent. The underlying difference between behaviour that creates awesome results and behaviour that creates undesirable results is in the belief systems on which the behaviour is based. Our mind determines what behaviour is called for by considering what it believes to be true in any given situation. One important factor our mind considers is whether a behaviour will result in pleasure or in pain.

Core beliefs — that is, beliefs formed early in our development that relate to what we think it takes to survive and get by in life — are continuously shaping our conscious thinking and our behaviour. A boss, parent or spouse with the core belief "I have to stay in control" will be no fun to work or live

5

with and will display behaviour that suppresses the creativity and self-expression of those around them.

## Fact 2

### WE CAN CHANGE OUR BELIEFS AND THEREBY CHANGE OUR BEHAVIOUR

Although our core beliefs are well and truly established, they can be changed. Once our core beliefs are formed, our minds interpret events and circumstances in accordance with them; you could say our minds actually search for evidence to prove our beliefs. However, we can take advantage of this very tendency to change our old beliefs and adopt new ones — by deciding what we *want* to believe and then deliberately interpreting events and circumstances accordingly and searching for evidence that our new beliefs are valid.

Once our beliefs change, our behaviour changes. If a tense, nervous person thoroughly implants in their mind the belief that it is always safe to relax, that is exactly what they will do.

## Fact 3

### WHEN OUR BELIEFS AND BEHAVIOUR CHANGE, THE RESULTS THEY PRODUCE ALSO CHANGE

We all know our behaviour produces physical results. The act of chopping up firewood generates chunks of the right size for the log burner. The behaviour of waking up each morning and saying to your partner, "Good morning. You're such a wonderful person — I love you," is going to produce quite different results over time from waking up and complaining about your partner's laziness.

## Fact 4

### WE HAVE A VIRTUALLY UNLIMITED ABILITY TO LEARN AND GROW

We do not start out with the knowledge necessary to create

our ideal life; it is something we accrue through self-awareness, study and questioning. Life is indeed a journey of learning and growing, and there are no known boundaries. We have it within us to produce whatever results we are after.

## *Fact 5*

### LIMITATIONS ARE LARGELY SELF-IMPOSED AND BASED ON FEAR

The biggest obstacles to the realisation of our dreams are our own disempowering beliefs, many of which express fear of some kind, and consequent behaviour. If I hadn't questioned my fears about writing this book — "I can't really do it", "No-one will be interested", "Everyone will laugh" — it would never have been written. Without the courage to dream and the commitment to making your dream a reality by over-coming your fears, you will remain where you are.

## *Fact 6*

### FEAR IS A BELIEF; IT ONLY EXISTS WHEN WE BELIEVE IT EXISTS

Fears must be believed in to have any power, yet when we examine our fears closely, we realise what little foundation they have. Fear of failure, being rejected, appearing a fool, making a mistake, not being good enough — these fears do not make sense when examined from the perspective of what it means to be human.

Time and time again I have done something I have feared to do, and as soon as I have done it the fear has evaporated. By consistently challenging fear, it loses its power over us.

It is indeed realistic for us to live our dreams, as is demon-strated by the many people who are already living theirs to-day or have done so in the past. To be realistic, though, we must base our decisions on facts, not on fear. However, we often use the term "realistic" in a disempowering manner. We say, for example, "I have to be realistic, I don't have the experience." But is experience something we can get? On reflection most people would agree that it is. We might also say we lack the necessary skills, don't have the "right" background, lack the time or money, don't get the support we need, or are without creative talent. What we are really saying is, "Yes but..." Don't get stuck in the "Yes but..." trap. Instead of justifying your fears, learn to question them.

What we create and achieve in our lives is dependent on the strategies we use, and with the right strategies we can create any results we want. Part III examines in detail how we can change our thoughts and feelings and move beyond our fears. If we let it, fear can stop us creating what we really want. Fear of failing or not making it, fear of change, fear of success, fear of loss, rejection or disapproval, fear of not having our needs met and missing out — all these can be overcome.

Your relationships, your health, your finances, the work you do, your living environment can all be as you would really like them to be. If you want to experience a wonderful loving relationship, you can do that. If you want to enjoy life in general more fully, you can do that. By conceiving an experience of life that really excites you, you are taking the first step towards making it a reality.

# 2

## Self-esteem: for a firm foundation

*I* have met people who tell me they have high self-esteem, yet when I ask them if they are doing what they really want to be doing with their lives their answer is no. This tells me their self-esteem isn't as high as it could be.

Your income can be high, you can occupy a position of power and responsibility, you can be famous or well known, and still you can have low self-esteem. Some people say self-esteem isn't a concern of theirs and shy away from the subject, as if to consider it would expose all manner of nasty things in themselves they would rather not know about. If you want to improve the quality of your life, however, it is *absolutely vital* self-esteem becomes a concern of yours.

Why is this? Because no part of your life can escape the powerful influence of your level of self-esteem. This is the foundation upon which you construct your life. If it is strong, you will have the confidence to explore your world. If it is weak, you will be fearful of venturing forth. To appreciate this it is necessary to understand how high self-esteem manifests itself.

*High self-esteem is accepting yourself, forgiving yourself and loving yourself — even when life isn't going your way.* Let's face it, things don't always work out as we plan, and when we have low self-esteem these incidents tend to hit us hard, sending us into a downward spiral and diminishing our resourcefulness and effectiveness. High self-esteem allows us to feel secure in ourselves no matter what is going on around us.

*High self-esteem is having a willingness to admit personal faults and do something about changing them.* We wouldn't be able to change and grow if we were unwilling to admit there are aspects of ourselves that need changing and improving.

*High self-esteem is not taking criticism to heart.* With low self-esteem, personal criticism can seem like a crippling blow. It is vital that we are able to accept criticism, to dismiss it if it is merely a projection of the critic's own insecurities, or to take action to rectify the fault without feeling there is something wrong with us.

*High self-esteem is having the ability to stand up for what you believe in when the situation calls for it.* Experiments conducted by a number of social psychologists indicate a surprising tendency for people to agree with group opinion even if what is being expressed is at odds with their own values or obviously untrue. This readiness to conform is apparent even when there is no evident benefit to be had from doing so, no overt pressure to comply, no threat of reproach or reprisal for thinking or acting independently. If we do not develop inner strength, external influences can override our inner convictions. A lack of courage to stand up for what one believes indicates a lack of self-esteem. Not surprisingly, the inclination to conform goes hand in hand with insecurity about one's own judgement and ideas. When people lack a sense of self-assurance and independence, they suppress their own beliefs and adopt those of the group to avoid alienation, being disliked and feeling they are wrong.

*High self-esteem is having the ability to communicate what you want and expect from others, and what you are willing to give in return, in a way that ensures everyone wins.* Life is about relationships; from doing the grocery shopping or having your car repaired to running a business or interacting with your family, you are constantly engaging in relationships. Your level of self-esteem determines how effectively you are able to participate and communicate in these.

*High self-esteem is believing you are worth the time and effort it takes to decide what in your heart you really want, to plan your future and to focus on its realisation.* People with low self-esteem simply don't believe they're worth the effort involved or able to create the results they know they would like.

*High self-esteem is expecting the best as defined by your own values.* People with low self-esteem accept less than they want, believing they are undeserving or uncreative.

*High self-esteem is accepting you are sometimes wrong.* People with low self-esteem hate being wrong about anything because they think it means they are deficient. This breeds a defensive "I know it all" attitude which inhibits learning. Learning is something people with high self-esteem value, and the lessons to be taken from making mistakes are an important element in the learning process.

*High self-esteem is a feeling of worth independent of financial and material circumstances and the opinions of others.* People with low self-esteem commonly attempt to boost their sense of personal worth by surrounding themselves with the things to which those they know, or society at large, have attributed value or status, such as the "right" kind of car or home, or a job and level of income that put them on a par with others. There is every reason to draw pleasure and satisfaction from such things, but to consider them a measure of self-worth is to leave oneself exposed to the risk of feeling worthless should one have the misfortune to lose them. If your feelings about yourself are linked to external circumstances in this way and those circumstances change or threaten to do so, you are likely to experience emotional turmoil. The same applies if your sense of self-worth is dependent on others liking you.

*High self-esteem is having the courage to try something new, knowing you may not get it right at the first attempt.* Whatever you want from life, the chances are there will be many new challenges. High self-esteem plays an important role in achievement of all kinds.

11

Why, then, is self-esteem so important? Because your level of self-esteem determines the extent to which you embrace life and the degree of pleasure, happiness, self-expression, achievement and fulfilment you are able to experience. *Whether or not you go for what you want in life is determined by your level of self-esteem.*

High self-esteem is fundamental to mental, emotional, physical and spiritual wellbeing. A powerful sense of solidity accompanies high self-esteem, which makes you feel secure in yourself. High self-esteem is not dependent on the approval of others. When you have high self-esteem your fears become something you can learn from and you have a confidence and faith in yourself that is not easily shaken. With high self-esteem comes the ability to maintain a strong sense of self-love, self-appreciation and self-worth, no matter in what circumstances you find yourself. In a spiritual sense we are all equal and share the same source; on this level one human is considered neither less nor more than another, and it is on this level, ultimately, that high self-esteem operates.

It is impossible to overemphasise the importance of self-esteem to a happy and fulfilling life. In order to develop high self-esteem you must follow your true self, make up your own mind and decide on your own direction. You must explore, express and expand.

## *Beliefs: the building blocks of self-esteem*

Our beliefs determine our thoughts, feelings, expectations, standards and values. These in turn determine the decisions we make, the actions we take and the behaviour we adopt and display. The value of raising our self-esteem becomes evident when we realise that beliefs determine our behaviour in this way and that low self-esteem consists of a set of disempowering beliefs that cause us to act in disempowering ways.

Beliefs are the building blocks with which we fashion and mould our lives, and the beliefs that have the greatest impact on our lives are those that determine our level of self-esteem. These beliefs determine our ability and willingness to receive. What we believe we deserve, whether in terms of love, support, possessions, money, level of achievement, quality of environment and even health, is based on the worth and value that we attribute to ourselves. Our self-esteem beliefs influence whether we set goals or not and what type of goals these are. The extent to which we tap into our potential, the quality of our personal relationships, and our experience of life and the world in general all depend on our beliefs. It is these that determine how eager we are to embrace life.

If you wish to develop high self-esteem and resourceful states of mind, you must adopt empowering beliefs. The first thing you need to know to turn low self-esteem into high self-esteem is that *self-esteem is a belief system*. The second thing you need to know is that *belief systems can be changed* (as is explained later).

## *Do you have low self-esteem?*

Low self-esteem isn't something that affects only a few people. It is of epidemic proportions in the Western culture. It could even be called "normal". In the same way that pollution is a by-product of a dysfunctional system of using and managing resources, and that cancer is the consequence of a dysfunctional system of living, so low self-esteem is the result of a system or strategy of child rearing that disempowers the child and, subsequently, the adult the child becomes. An out-of-balance system produces out-of-balance results, and low self-esteem is one such result.

Low self-esteem is a dis-ease, just as surely as pollution or cancer is a dis-ease. An organism is open to disease when its immunity has been weakened. Low self-esteem can only exist when we are disassociated from the love that sustains us. When we believe in powerlessness, persecution and separation and are ignorant of our own power to create, we experience a state of fear. Weakened by fear we seem to be at

13

the mercy of a hostile universe, yet in truth we are creating our experiences every step of the way.

One of the effects of low self-esteem is the suppression of aliveness and the introduction of fear into the psyche. Is the suppression of aliveness natural? Is it natural to live in fear? And if so, why is it that so many people — and the numbers are constantly increasing — are intent on experiencing and expressing more of their aliveness and ridding themselves of fear? Add to this the fact that both these desires seem to spring from individuals' own intuitive thinking and feeling, and it would seem that humanity's most basic and natural drive is to experience more aliveness, in which high self-esteem plays a vital part. Low self-esteem may unfortunately be normal, but it is only natural to the extent that pollution is natural.

Low self-esteem results from disempowering beliefs and behaviour that have become a conditioned part of us. Beliefs and the behaviour they motivate produce very specific results, and this makes low self-esteem very easy to identify. Some of these results are listed below in the form of questions. If you answer yes to any of these, you can be sure that, no matter how good your life currently is, it can be even better, and you are going to benefit tremendously from a boost to your self-esteem.

*Answering yes to any of the following indicates low self-esteem:*

• Are you living a life that taps into only a fraction of your full potential?

• Do you have dreams that you have put aside?

• Do you sometimes feel there is something wrong with you, or that you are guilty, even when it doesn't seem logical to feel that way?

• Do you think of yourself as uncreative?

• Do you have a hard time figuring out what your true feelings are?

• Do you hold back from asking for what you want for fear of hurting others?

- Do you hide your aliveness and excitement?
- Do you say yes when you want to say no, and vice versa?
- Have you achieved a lot but still feel unsatisfied and that there is something missing in your life?
- Do you settle for less than you really want and then justify doing so?
- Do you give up on what you want when others disapprove?
- Do you feel you deserve more encouragement, love and support from your relationships?
- Are you working at a job you don't enjoy just for the money?
- Do you put your emotional, physical or spiritual well-being to one side in order to handle more "important" things?
- Do fear and anxiety stop you from doing things you want to do?
- Do you experience a mental block when thinking about what you really want out of life?
- Are you doing things you don't want to do?

Feeling anxious at the thought of expressing your aliveness, or guilty when you are having fun; constantly condemning yourself for not being good enough, smart enough, attractive enough or for making mistakes; the detrimental effect all this has on your ability to achieve what you want — such is the price to be paid for having low self-esteem.

You can start developing high self-esteem right now by implementing the ideas discussed in this book. Question what is normal, break the bonds of the past, claim your uniqueness and be yourself.

# 3

## Our natural drives:
## the essence of self-esteem

*T*HREE powerful drives — the drive to explore, the drive to express and the drive to expand — represent the moving force in our lives. These drives are a manifestation of our life urge. Allowing them to assert themselves brings immense power, pleasure and happiness.

To give these natural drives full rein is to follow one's true self. To suppress them is to create pain and low self-esteem. They are evolutionary forces constantly seeking an outlet. They are the essence of change, the foundation of growth. Their release is a prerequisite to high self-esteem, essential to personal evolution.

### The drive to explore

We all have a powerful curiosity inside us. We want to understand ourselves and know who we are. We want to explore what we are capable of and how to get what we desire. We want to know what works and what doesn't. We want to test our limits and then test them again.

Whenever we ask a question, we are exploring. We want to know something we don't already know. It's natural for children to ask questions. Isn't it true that they just keep pouring them out one after the other? "Why do you do that?" "What's this for?" "How come they do that?" "How does this work?"

Did you ask questions like these as a child? Were your parents' responses empowering or disempowering? Unfortunately, many parents' responses to their children's curiosity are less than supportive. Their children's drive to explore becomes suppressed. Many stop exploring or contain their exploration within restrictive and "safe" limits. If you stopped exploring, do you think you would continue to grow at the same speed? Do you think you would grow at all? Would you pick up a book such as this? Would you even visit a book shop? What chance do you think you would have of developing interests or hobbies? Without exploring would you be able to develop a skill? Ask yourself right now, "What cost am I paying in my life for not exploring?" When the desire to explore becomes suppressed, the quality of life deteriorates.

 *Why is it that when someone steps out of line there's a rush to get him back in, instead of an interest in where he is going?*

Barry Stevens

Take a moment to consider the impact that doubling or even tripling the amount of exploring you do would have on your life. Do you think you would experience more personal power? How do you think it might affect the quality of your life? Do you think you would experience more pleasure and excitement? You can be sure you would.

The desire to explore springs naturally from inside you. Follow your curiosity. Explore your capabilities and creativity. Align yourself with this driving force within you by asking yourself exploratory questions. What can you do to transform the quality of your life? Where do you want to be in five years' time and when are you going to get started? What new things do you want to experience? What have you always wanted to do but have been putting off? How much more are you capable of? How can you become more creative and more effective? Learning to ask questions of this kind is a powerful way to reawaken your drive to explore. To find out what you really want in life you must explore.

17

*The quality of your life is directly related to your exploration of life.* By asking questions you will focus your mind on the possibilities, opening up vast areas you may not have been aware of or have forgotten existed. As the picture widens, a sense of excitement will develop, and through excitement you will experience pleasure. The key to creating high self-esteem and the experience of pleasure is to align yourself with who you already are, your true self.

 In the important decisions of personal life, we should be governed, I think, by the deep inner needs of our nature

Sigmund Freud

## *The drive to express*

This is the force that drives us to create, whether the creation be art or technology or a home and family. It motivates us to share our love, ideas and talents, to build a business, to shape our environment. The drive to express is about taking action. It gives form to the creative life force that runs through us. This drive is inseparable from being human; without it we would not exist. The simple fact that we are alive is a demonstration of this drive. It is the force that causes us to grow from an embryo into an adult human being.

Think of young children and how they spontaneously express themselves as they reach out and explore the world around them. A child does not have to be taught to be alive, but through childhood conditioning our drive to express ourselves can become associated with pain. If a child's exuberance, vitality and spontaneous expression of aliveness are discouraged by overdiscipline, the child will learn to inhibit its life urge and avoid such experiences. Even though such early suppression of our aliveness can change the direction our lives take, however, our ability to express ourselves is still present within us and can be brought back to life. By changing our beliefs we can unleash our creative, self-expressive power. The drive to express ourselves is primal and cannot be lost.

> Perhaps we shall soon be able to use as our guide and model the fully growing and self-fulfilling human being, the one in whom all his potentialities are coming to full development, the one whose inner nature expresses itself freely, rather than being warped, suppressed, or denied
>
> Abraham Maslow

You can develop the courage to communicate your wants, expectations and boundaries and your feelings about the things that are important to you. Your ability to communicate is a key indicator of your level of self-esteem. With high self-esteem you won't hold back from sharing your ideas and experiences, and you will feel confident and safe being seen and heard. You won't be afraid to question the validity of the rules and opinions of authority. With high self-esteem you can express your need for support without feeling resentful, ashamed or that your power is being diminished. Asking for help in no way implies one is inadequate. With high self-esteem you can express your aliveness spontaneously and passionately.

The same expressive drive is present in nature. A seed is saying (figuratively), "I want a chance to express myself. I want to grow." And it does grow, from a tiny seed into a huge tree. When the tree is chopped back to a stump, it puts forth new shoots. Nature's desire to grow and express itself is unstoppable. Plants grow out of tiny cracks in the side of city buildings and force their way through concrete sidewalks. Just as a tree's nature is to grow and express itself, so too is ours.

How you define yourself has a powerful impact on how you express yourself. When your definition of yourself represents a proclamation of your individuality, you are choosing

19

to live in your own unique way. You are self-defined when you make your own choices and consciously choose your own beliefs, behaviour, values, standards and life direction. You can use the principles outlined in this book to define yourself in a way that fits how you really want to express yourself, that supports your personal vision of an ideal life and has you charging towards its realisation.

## *The drive to expand*

This is the growth force, whether emotional, mental, physical or spiritual growth. It is the impetus behind the drives to explore and express. Everything is impelled to expand: cells multiply, populations increase, knowledge and understanding grow. On an experiential level, whatever we consistently focus our attention on expands. *The more we focus our thoughts on something, the more we experience it.* If our thoughts are consistently of a resentful nature, we will experience increasing resentment and draw to ourselves a steady stream of circumstances to be resentful of. The process will be the same if we adopt a more empowering outlook, but of course the result will be contrastingly beneficial.

> We have pushed so much of our life away, held it captive so deep within us that when we begin to let go we notice how much our expectations, concepts, and preconceptions have limited our experience
>
> Stephen Levine

When you feel that you want to be more than you currently are and to take your understanding to a higher level, you are feeling the push of this powerful drive. Sharing and giving are also an expression of this drive, an example being when you feel the need to connect and deepen your bond with others and to experience a greater sense of oneness with all things. How can I share what I know with others so they can benefit too? How can I help others improve the quality of their lives as I have improved that of mine? What can I give? These are the types of questions this drive motivates us to ask.

We are *internally motivated* to expand our experience of pleasure, happiness and love. When we want to break out of feelings of restriction and to experience freedom, we are feeling the pull of our drive to expand. Holding on, either physically — with tension — or mentally — by refusing to be flexible in our thinking — is working in direct opposition to this drive.

Start increasing your aliveness now. Align yourself with the natural drives to explore, express and expand. High self-esteem is dependent on having these drives operating freely in your life.

## *The search for aliveness*

The drive to explore, the drive to express and the drive to expand are the forces through which we search for an experience of aliveness. Our desire to experience pleasure and our search for aliveness are one. Exploring, expressing and expanding are all experiences of aliveness. Beyond the search for meaning in life, we are surely searching for just such an experience. The only thing that *is* meaningful is aliveness, and being fully alive is all that we really want. When we experience aliveness we feel fulfilled.

If you open yourself to the motivation of the drives to explore, express and expand, and learn to follow the internal guidance of your intuition, you will discover a form of self-expression that gives you that experience of aliveness, and you will naturally want to direct your energies into this. In doing so you will feel a renewed passion and excitement for life well up spontaneously inside you, and you will find your self-esteem increasing naturally.

On the other hand, how can you hope to build a solid experience of self-esteem, of respecting and accepting yourself, if you fail to do what, in your heart, you are compelled to do? Suppress or deny your inner guidance and deep down you will hate yourself for it. By not picking up a paintbrush when you have the urge to be a painter, by not enrolling at university when you are drawn to further learning, by not setting sail when you have a desire to travel the world's oceans, by not speaking up when you know there is injustice, you will feel unworthy and unable to respect yourself. The desires that spring from your deeper nature are expressions of your aliveness; suppressing or denying them is suppressing or denying life.

*To have a lasting experience of aliveness we must follow our true selves.* Some people describe it as following their bliss, passion or heart. Whatever you call it, the message is the same. Do what is *intuitively* in you to do; this is how you will find your aliveness. How to move towards a more intuitive way of living is the subject of the next chapter.

# 4

## *End internal war:*
## *use your whole brain*

*T*HE human brain can be viewed in terms of two contrast-
ing functions.

First, there are the functions of analysing, applied in the
processing of language and figures and in the use of logic,
which we attribute to the left portion of the brain. The left
brain tends towards conformity and prefers structure. It sets
rigid rules and likes working by them. It fears being out of
control, and demands reasons for everything. The left brain
also functions rather like a controlling, dominating parent,
giving orders, criticising, condemning and judging.

Second, there are the functions of intuition and instinct,
attributed to the right side of the brain. This half of the brain
likes to function freely, discovering through exploration and
imagery, choosing its own direction, thoughts and behaviour
rather than following the common path. It represents
individuality and is guided by its own views rather than
externally produced views. The right brain values creativity
and operates with a sense of timelessness; it enjoys looking at
the big-picture perspective. You may have noticed when you
have been involved in a creative project that you have become
lost in what you are doing, losing track of time and forgetting
to stop to eat. Five hours go past and it feels like one. This is
the right brain in action. It relates to things as they are in the
present moment. It experiences and responds with feelings
and is quite comfortable operating on a "gut" level.

The problem is that through our conditioning, both in the family, where so much focus is placed on survival and "making a living", and in society at large, where we tend to conform to avoid isolation and alienation, our right brain functions are suppressed. Creativity is in danger of being extinguished in Western culture. We are predominantly left brain functioning. We learn not to value functions such as imagination, creativity and feelings, and anyone who displays these is labelled "special" or "genius" if they are popular or "weird" if they are not, which is quite incorrect.

In the workplace, both clerical and factory jobs entail a great number of menial tasks. It is a minority of people who are in such a position that they get to think creatively. Even in management, creativity and innovation are largely lost under the pressure to maintain profitability. At school the pressure to perform, do better than fellow students and conform to a curriculum often biased towards outdated ideas, guarantees that creativity, which demands a relaxed, cooperative and unrestrained environment to thrive, is restricted. We have become divorced from the natural creative process of food production, forgetting that the vegetables we purchase in the supermarket started out as seeds in the ground. TV and video offer us entertainment that is more and more compelling, conditioning us to demand ever higher levels of arousal. Our own creative resources seem mundane and insignificant by comparison. Creativity becomes external, something that happens "out there", something that other people do.

A major step towards expressing your true self is to start thinking of yourself as creative, because the truth is that you are, like it or not.

 *People tend not to trust their gut instincts enough*

Anita Roddick

Our creativity is crying out for expression, but our left brain logic dampens it down with beliefs such as, "I'm not good enough", "It's not safe" and "I can't trust." We have a mini war going on inside our heads between our left and right brain. Self-esteem is dependent on an inner acceptance, and we cannot have that if there's an internal war being fought between different aspects of ourselves. When we split off from and judge other aspects of ourselves, we are creating the conditions necessary for low self-esteem. High self-esteem is dependent on a whole brain experience. Our left brain logic argues that even though we are constantly improving we are never good enough. It judges our performance in sports, work, relationships, etc. as inadequate and constantly fights to implement the things it believes are necessary if we are to improve. The right brain does not judge. In a sense the use of drugs and alcohol is an attempt to suppress the left brain's chatter and judgements and to retreat into the pleasure of right brain acceptance.

In essence we have largely suppressed one half of our way of knowing and experiencing ourselves and the world. Culturally we learn to pay attention to what is said rather than what is felt. Creative functions don't operate by following the rules; by definition creativity must break these. Yet our left brain loves and needs rules, and since following the rules is the more socially acceptable mode of operation we end up relying on left brain analytical skills and judge our creative, intuitive selves.

The left brain tends to override and suppress the creative and emotional right brain, reasoning that doing so keeps us out of trouble — which, during childhood, may have been true. The right brain seems to take on the role of the abused inner child. It's the part of us that doesn't get to paint, draw, express or have its feelings validated. It can feel scary expressing our creative, intuitive selves, to follow our own inner sense of direction, to let go of control and preconceptions of good and bad, right and wrong, black and white, when doing so has been associated with punishment and the withdrawal of love and spiritual nourishment.

*To get more out of your life, get more out of your brain.* When you deny those creative, intuitive functions attributed to your right brain, you deny yourself half of the richness of existence. The full use of all mental functions is necessary if one is to feel fulfilled. The ideal is to have both sides of the brain working equally so they support each other. Create a supportive, interactive relationship between your logical and intuitive selves.

> I am convinced that human continuance now depends entirely upon: The individual's integrity of speaking and acting only on the individual's own within-self-intuited and reasoned initiative
>
> R. Buckminster Fuller

Learn to listen to your right brain intuition and use your left brain logic to back up with action what your intuition tells you. To discover the direction in which your true self wants to go, you *must* learn to listen to your intuition. The questions, "What do I really want to be doing now?", "What do I have a passion for?", "What can I do that will increase my experience of aliveness?" must first be answered intuitively. Intuition balanced with reason is the key to following your true self.

By spending more time in your right brain you can have a greater experience of wholeness, acceptance and gratitude. Take a holiday with your right brain. Meditate, visualise, use your imagination, be in nature, explore art, learn to play a musical instrument or pursue other creative ventures. One way to tap into your intuition is to ask yourself questions without looking for an immediate answer. Instead, wait for the answer to come through your intuition. When I set a goal, I often ask myself what it is I need to know to guarantee reaching it. Sometimes it takes a few hours for an intuitive answer to come to me; on other occasions it takes a day or even a week. I have learnt to trust my intuition, and the answer always comes. You can derive great benefit from using your intuition in this way in all areas of your life. In the case of finance, for example, you can ask, "What do I need to do to reach my financial goals for this year?" In a relationship you can ask, "What can I do to experience more love with this person?" Often you will get more than one answer; you can then use your left brain logic to choose the one you like the most, or go with your right brain and choose the one that feels the best, or make a choice that is a balance of both.

A whole brain perspective provides a new frame of reference and opens the way to new solutions for boosting self-esteem. By developing your creative drives, intuitive thinking, emotional responses and an attitude of acceptance, you are healing the split between your left and right brain and at the same time raising your self-esteem.

# Part II

# *The bonds of the past*

# 5

## The shaping of beliefs

### The first nine months

*T*HE womb may seem a strange place to start when considering the shaping of our beliefs and the behaviour that springs from them, particularly when we don't remember the time we spent there, but there is a steadily growing awareness of the impact our time in the womb — and, later, our birth experience — can have.

It is now understood that our lives are sustained by energy, and that life is essentially an energy experience. All communication is based on a transference of energy, regardless of its form; a tribal drum, a satellite, a computer network or human speech are all reliant upon energy. Humans are energy transmitters and receivers. When a mother *receives* communication from her environment, her baby, by being present in her womb, is a party to that information. The baby is also a party to any communication the mother *transmits,* including emotional responses. Whatever energy the mother experiences is built into the baby's make-up; therefore what the mother experiences has the potential to have a significant impact upon her offspring.

If your mother was constantly stressed, worried, upset or depressed, or had persistent feelings of guilt, fear, sadness or anger, while you were in her womb, these energies will have been an integral part of your building material. Your mother's experience will have been your experience. Even in the womb, conditioning is taking place. We become accustomed to specific feelings that later form expectations; we expect to experience the same feelings. All the feelings we experience in the womb — anxiety, pleasure, fear, joy, stress — become associated with the comfort, warmth and safety of the womb. They become comfortable and familiar to us.

The womb experience creates a mix of beliefs and feelings; some become constant companions throughout life, while others are triggered by specific stimuli, just as in the mother's case. If during pregnancy your mother was overly concerned that something may have been wrong with you, as many mothers are (especially with their first child), you might well have an underlying sense yourself that there is something essentially wrong with you. Although this is not the only cause of this type of feeling, it is an important one to consider.

What was your mother experiencing while you were in the womb? If possible, have a chat with her about it. Did her life at that time contain emotional or financial stress? What were her feelings about carrying you? Was she worried about a painful birth or did she harbour concerns for your health? If your mother had expectations that created anxiety, these may now be influencing you. In the case of a mother who feels guilty for being pregnant and at first tries to hide the baby's presence, that baby can grow up feeling guilty for existing.

One effective way of becoming aware of the expectations that develop during our time in the womb (as well as during birth, dealt with in the following section) is a simple process called rebirthing. Rebirthing brings to conscious awareness early, buried convictions we have formed about ourselves, and often a memory of when these were bred. It is a personal transformation technique that uses a specific method of breathing called connected breathing, along with total relaxation (it usually takes place lying down) and a focus on what is being experienced in the body.

Connected breathing entails inhaling and exhaling in an uninterrupted in–out rhythm. In other words, the moment the exhale is complete, the inhale begins; the moment the inhale is complete, the exhale begins. There are no pauses or gaps, no holding on — just a continuous cycle of steady breathing performed in a very relaxed manner.

Limiting conclusions about life, the origins of which stretch back to our earliest experiences, although held subconsciously, inhibit the flow of our energy or aliveness. They cause us, even though we are unaware of the fact, to hold on mentally, to tighten up physically and to restrict our breathing. Connected breathing increases the amount of energy in the body, which has the effect of bringing to awareness the beliefs that are limiting the extent to which we embrace life. You could say the effect of rebirthing is similar to the way in which a committed, loving relationship causes an observant, growth-oriented couple to become aware of the resistances to and fears of experiencing deeper intimacy. The difference, though — and one of the reasons why rebirthing is so effective — is that you do not have to think about it or figure anything out; the increased energy flow created by the breathing does all the work of transforming the mind. What actually takes place during rebirthing is the process of perturbation — the subject of chapter 12.

Rebirthing helps one become aware of fears of and resistances to a deeper experience of aliveness. At the same time, by experiencing and accepting the various feelings that accompany a rebirthing session, one integrates fear and resistance permanently into a profound global appreciation of life.

In the course of teaching rebirthing, I have met and worked with many people who have traced the source of self-doubts and fears that contributed to low self-esteem back to their time in the womb. The following account, of Jan's womb experience, illustrates the impact this time of life can have on an adult.

Two weeks into Jan's mother's pregnancy a close member of her family died, traumatising her. Two weeks later another member of the family died, causing more trauma. On both occasions Jan's mother believed the pregnancy had ended. As an adult, Jan noticed that two weeks after the conception of a new relationship, and again at four weeks, she would expect some sort of trauma to bring an end to it. When this didn't happen, her expectation was so strong that she would create a trauma. As a result, a great number of Jan's relationships in fact lasted only two or four weeks.

## *Birth: our first roller-coaster ride*

Our nine months in the womb come to an abrupt end at birth. Birth is the first major transition in our lives, and it isn't always a smooth one. We are thrust from the warm, dark, safe environment inside our mother's body into the confusing, demanding and confronting external environment.

Birth can be an overpowering experience which overloads us with stimulation. We can experience feelings of pressure, fear, pain and panic, and distress at the separation from our source of nourishment and our comfortable home. Light and sound are strong and direct, touch can seem rough. With the cord being cut and the do-or-die first breath, the whole thing can add up to a potentially traumatic experience. It can be perceived by a newborn infant as an ordeal of physical attack and abuse. The sensations are all new; never before in our nine months of life have we experienced so much violent change.

As early as 1909 Sigmund Freud pointed out that the process of birth is the source of, and model for, the experience of anxiety. One cannot deny that an event of this magnitude will leave a lasting impression. Otto Rank, a colleague of Freud's, took this concept even further, establishing birth trauma as the central emotional factor in future psychological development. Rank believed the trauma of birth was the starting point from which all future human development proceeded.

*Since birth is our first experience of change, it becomes the model for our future expectations of change.* All the emotion linked to birth is also linked to change. When we encounter subsequent situations involving change, the same emotional responses of helplessness, fear and the sense of being overpowered are evoked. Changing jobs, leaving a relationship, moving home, being rejected — any experience in which we can perceive loss — can all produce these responses. Change becomes a feared experience and is perceived as painful. Our bottom-line fear becomes one of not surviving the impending change. The anxiety we link to the experience of change becomes an inducement to avoid situations involving change.

Not only is the basis of our future conception of change laid down at birth; the foundations of how we come to view ourselves, others and life in general are also put in place. Our birth trauma can result in our perceiving ourselves as guilty if, during the process, we sense we are causing our mother pain; also in believing we have to struggle to survive and in feeling that we aren't safe. These beliefs subsequently become generalised, and we apply them to all aspects of our lives. Life becomes a struggle, the world is viewed as unsafe, and guilt infiltrates our daily existence. The convictions we develop colour our perspective on life and contribute towards our experience of reality.

Our ability to integrate birth trauma depends to a large extent on the degree of care, love, nourishment, acceptance and encouragement our parents give us throughout infancy. In the absence of these things, the anxiety we experienced during birth and any disempowering perceptions that sprang therefrom become strengthened.

## *Conditioning after birth*

Throughout this book the focus is mostly on the influence family conditioning has on people's ability to create the kind of life they really want. Although cultural influences are important, I believe they are secondary to the influence of the family. Cultures are transformed by the people within them as they transform themselves. The beliefs and values of the young of today dictate the shape of society tomorrow. Society is a result, people are its cause. How we shape society, and society's ability to influence us, are determined by our core

beliefs about ourselves, formed during our earliest days —
beliefs about our worth as people, beliefs about our ability to
produce desirable results, beliefs about the value of our ideas,
and most importantly beliefs about our ability to function
independently of our parents and about the value of life.

Our ability to discriminate between what is desirable and
undesirable in the world around us depends on the degree
to which we were encouraged to think for ourselves during
childhood, as opposed to being taught merely to conform.
Our ability to take action to address that which we deem
undesirable depends on the degree to which we were encouraged to act on our own thinking.

## *Parents: our first teachers*

It is important to understand that when I refer to parents I do
not mean "bad" parents. Parents can be gentle, sensitive and
kind and still be, in effect, abusive towards their children,
calling what they do child rearing. Parents mistreat their children not because of their personality per se, but because they
were themselves mistreated as children and are repeating
learnt patterns of behaviour. It is also important to appreciate
that conditioning doesn't need to be violent or physically
abusive to produce low self-esteem. Conditioning can take
place in subtle and virtually undetectable ways.

Humankind is evolving, and with each successive generation our awareness of what it is to be human grows and
deepens. As people question the values, beliefs and behaviour of the generation before them and attempt to make wiser
choices in the upbringing and education of their children,
we move progressively towards a more loving and humane
attitude towards one another.

Throughout childhood our parents are our mentors and
our protectors; they are our source of love and nourishment;
they have the power to give and the power to take away;
they have the power to bestow affection and the power to
inflict pain. Without being aware of it they also possess, and

consistently employ, some of the most powerful and effective conditioning techniques known. It is through their application of these that, as children, we learn.

## Modelling

We learn in the first instance by imitating, or modelling, others. Our parents represent high-status models, so we look up to them and copy their behaviour, even if it is disempowering. Our parents are the model we use to learn how things are done; they are the objects of our "how to be" study.

A child watches Dad using a hammer and does not miss a chance to pick the hammer up himself and give the same task a go. A young boy I know not yet attending school has become quite a handyman through modelling his father. A young girl modelling her own interaction with her mother sternly tells her doll off for misbehaving, spanks its bottom and orders it to go to its room. She then turns to play with Teddy because he's been a "good Teddy". Because of the length of time we are able to study our parents, and the amount of repetition involved, we have the opportunity to make in-depth observations. We come to know intimately the ins and outs of every behaviour, strategy, belief and feeling our parents have. We get to know in precise detail how they handle every situation in which they find themselves, how they get into and out of a given situation.

Even though we may not demonstrate that we've learnt so much about our parents' behaviour at the time, the behaviour itself, and the situations and environments in which it has occurred, have been committed to memory. Later we recreate the same situations without being aware of doing so, unconsciously acting out the modelled behaviour. Some of the behaviour we model from our parents we may not use until we have our own children.

This extract from psychoanalyst Alice Miller's book *For Your Own Good* is a powerful statement on the modelling of disempowering behaviour:

...when children are trained, they learn how to train others in turn. Children who are lectured to, learn how to lecture; if they are admonished, they learn how to admonish; if scolded, they learn how to scold; if ridiculed, they learn how to ridicule; if humiliated, they learn how to humiliate; if their psyche is killed, they will learn how to kill — the only question is who will be killed: oneself, others, or both.*

This learning may be unconscious, but it takes place nonetheless. While you were a child what beliefs did your parents demonstrate? If parents' dreams are never realised, if they never attain the happiness or achieve the goals they want in life, their belief in their inability to get what they want becomes their children's belief in *their* inability to get what *they* want. We have hopes and dreams just as our parents did, and we can find ourselves unable to fulfil them because we have unconsciously modelled the same strategies our parents used, strategies that may be less than optimally effective. We often develop an expectation, although we may not be fully conscious of it, that what is true of our parents' lives will be true of our own. We have dreams, yet we expect them to remain unfulfilled. Unfortunately for many, "I can't get what I want" becomes a code by which they live.

What degree of love and affection did your parents bestow? Did they evince struggle or fear? Did you model this? We model our parents' level of self-esteem. This cannot be hidden from view — the fears, self-doubts and disempowering beliefs that make up low self-esteem are demonstrated in the way people talk and behave, in their body language and how they live in general. The beliefs, behaviour, values and expectations of our parents become the basis of our own.

Why do parents set the particular examples that they do, some of which disempower us and create low self-esteem? Because they teach us what they learnt from observing the behaviour of their own parents, the bad along with the good. *Parents teach the only model they have,* and we end up on the receiving end of their abusiveness as well as their tenderness. We all teach what we believe to be true. If our parents had

*For Your Own Good: Hidden cruelty in child-rearing and the roots of violence*, Farrar Straus Giroux, New York, 1988

themselves been taught in a different way by their parents, they would have taught us that way. If they learnt new ideas through self-education, we will have been exposed to them too.

## *Repetition*

Subsequent to modelling, our thinking and behaviour are shaped by the power of repetition. Our parents provide role models, which we imitate. They continue to provide them, and we continue to imitate. Repetition reinforces the lesson. If you want to master something, regardless of whether it's a musical instrument, a martial art or making movies, how do you do it? You practise — over and over again. So it is with behaviour. Eventually you don't even have to think about what you are doing because it becomes internalised and second nature.

If you left home at the age of 16, you had nearly 16 years' repetition of parental rules, day after day. How well do you think you would be able to play the piano after 16 years' daily practise, starting at a very early age when your mind was fresh and hungry for information and experience? The chances are you would have pretty well mastered the instrument.

Most people are masters of low self-esteem. Our behaviour and beliefs are moulded through the repetitive experience of disapproval or approval, pain or pleasure. Each successive repetition strengthens our memory and thus our learning. Repetition is powerful on its own, but when allied with other learning methods, its power to condition becomes awesome.

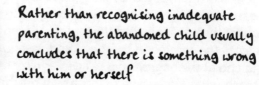

Rather than recognising inadequate parenting, the abandoned child usually concludes that there is something wrong with him or herself

Lucia Capacchione

## *Association*

The third factor influencing the beliefs and behaviour we adopt is the associations we make. Everything we experience we give meaning to. We make decisions as to what things represent depending on what they are associated with. For instance, we have seen how the pain of birth is also the pain of a great change. Through association, any change can become linked to that pain. The reason so many people resist new ideas and new technology is the negative associations they make with change.

If someone close to us dies, we feel sadness because we associate death with loss. However, there are cultures that celebrate death, that perceive it as a great honour and associate it with returning to the source of one's being. Death is seen not as an end to life but as a continuation of life on a higher level.

When we behave in such a way as to incur punishment or the withdrawal of our parents' love — both experiences of pain — we quickly learn two things: first, to associate such behaviour with being punished; second, to refrain from that behaviour to avoid punishment. As long as that behaviour remains associated with punishment, we will refrain. One soon learns not to run up to a dog and hug it after being bitten a few times. By the same token, when we behave in a way that brings us love or reward, we quickly learn to make that association too.

Although we may not be consciously aware of it, we naturally form and remember associations or links between events, feelings, behaviour and the environment around us. We can associate being hit with pain, a certain look, a particular behaviour, a tone of voice, the words used and even the room or place in which we are hit. Advertisers often have great success in conditioning us to associate qualities such as ruggedness, charisma, intimacy, intelligence, sexiness, environmental concern, convenience and healthy living with their clients' products in the bid to motivate us to buy.

In fact, regardless of what it is, it is the associations we make with something that determine how we feel about it and what action we take. During my childhood, holidays were a time when the normal family tensions and conflicts were replaced by a relaxed, fun atmosphere. Because of this I learnt to associate holidays with great pleasure and, in many ways, have striven to make my whole life feel like a holiday. Maybe there is a song you associate with an old lover or special occasion, and every time you hear it memories of that person or occasion flood into your mind. We store in our memory whole sequences of events that form chains of association, and all it takes is stimulation of one link in the chain to spark off the whole thing. Never underestimate the power of association in the shaping of your thinking.

> Happily, it is possible to raise anyone's self-esteem, no matter what one's age or condition. Since the feeling of low worth has been learned, it can be unlearned, and something new learned in its place
>
> Virginia Satir

## Emotional intensity

The more emotionally intense an experience, the deeper the imprint it makes on the memory. We have vivid memories of events that were extremely exciting or traumatic. This is not to say that incidents we consider boring or mundane cannot make an equally deep impression — through repetition even the most insignificant experiences can become ingrained in the memory — but emotional intensity serves to speed up the learning process.

Which would be easier to recall in six months' time — a day sitting at home in the sun or a day at a fun park where you went for a hair-raising roller-coaster ride? Having all your senses stimulated at once increases both the strength of the memory and the chance of what you learn from the experience being retained for longer. Being told not to touch a hot stove may have little effect on your behaviour. If you burn yourself on the stove, however, the intensity of the experience, involving considerable pain, is likely to be such that you learn to refrain from touching the stove in future.

We aren't always conscious of what is stored in our mind, however. For example, when a memory is associated with excessive emotional pain it may be suppressed or pushed out of our awareness. Suppression of this kind is a function of our drive to avoid pain.

## *The drive to avoid pain*

Pain can be used as an extremely effective conditioning tool. It can be administered in the form of disapproval and reprimand, the withdrawal of affection or privileges, the denial of freedom, constant fault finding and criticism, verbal humiliation or shouting, smacking or beating — all these represent pain.

We can also experience or anticipate pain when we are on the receiving end of more covert behaviour, such as an angry or disapproving look, an aggressive or disapproving tone of voice, or abrupt physical movements. As young children we quickly interpret such behaviour as a sign of impending trouble. Our drive to avoid pain is such that we pick up the first hint of possible future pain. With practice we come to recognise a look or a change in the tone of a voice that signals pain and quickly modify our behaviour to avoid it. *Any behaviour we have linked to an experience of pain we are highly motivated to refrain from repeating.*

Social psychologist Neal Miller demonstrated how easily pain can be linked to an experience with the following experiment. Rats were placed in a white box in which they were given an electric shock. They learnt that by pressing a lever they could escape the box and avoid the shocks. Once they had learnt to do this, they were *never* shocked in the white box again. But by this time just the *sight* of the white box sent the rats into a frenzy, and on being placed in it they pressed the lever and made an escape as quickly as possible. The rats had learnt to associate the white box with an experience of pain.

Miller went on to make the lever inoperative and installed a wheel which opened the door instead. The rats, on discovering they could no longer leave the box by pressing the lever, tried frantically to escape by some other means, and many discovered that if they turned the wheel, the door would open. From then on, rats entering the white box bolted to the wheel and escaped to safety. Having found their initial learnt behaviour no longer produced the desired result, they had been motivated by the expectation and fear of pain to come up with a new behaviour that did.

What is significant is that in the end the pain was *only* an expectation for the rats, not a reality. If they had stayed in the box they would not have experienced another shock. A rat's drive to avoid pain is no different from our own drive. It is interesting to note just how easily conditioning of the kind demonstrated by Miller can take place. *Most of our fears in adult life are based on expectation and not reality.*

It is worth summing up the conclusions of Miller's experiment as they apply to ourselves:

1. An experience of pain can be remembered and form the *expectation* that similar pain will be experienced in a similar situation even if this is unlikely.

2. We will do our utmost to avoid an environment or situation that we have *associated* with pain.

3. If we find our behaviour ineffective in avoiding further pain, we will *change* it until we get the result we are after.

Our drive to avoid pain motivates us to avoid our own mental anxieties. *Cognitive dissonance* is a term used to describe the experience of mental anxiety or discomfort we experience when we find ourselves in, or confronted with, a situation we have associated with some form of distress. You will experience cognitive dissonance when:

1. You behave or contemplate behaving in a way you believe will lead to unpleasantness or unease. If you are a vegetarian, for example, the thought of going to work in a meat works will probably give you an experience of cognitive dissonance. If you believe that men or women reject you, contemplating asking someone out for a date will create cognitive dissonance. If you are used to a $200,000 annual income and believe that is the minimum necessary for you to survive, contemplating a drop to $30,000 will create cognitive dissonance. If you expect your behaviour to produce uncomfortable results, particularly over the long term, you will create cognitive dissonance and will be motivated to adopt alternative behaviour likely to bring about a more desirable outcome.

2. Someone else behaves in a manner that goes against your principles. An example would be if someone broke into your house. Such behaviour is at odds with most people's notions of respect for personal privacy, property and ownership. Inappropriate behaviour of this kind by others is likely to create cognitive dissonance in you.

3. You find yourself in a situation or environment that is at odds with your personal beliefs. In Neal Miller's experiment, the rats, having found they couldn't leave the box by pressing the lever and having learnt that the box was (according to previous experience at any rate) a painful place to be, underwent cognitive dissonance. If I asked you to walk across a rope bridge spanning a deep ravine, and you believed the bridge was old and obviously unsafe, you would experience cognitive dissonance or anxiety if you did my bidding. The behaviour of crossing the bridge would conflict with your belief that the bridge was unsafe. To reduce your anxiety you could either defend your belief that it wasn't safe to cross the bridge and refuse to do so, or you could change your beliefs so they supported you in crossing. For example, you could decide to believe that it was good to take the occasional risk, or that it would help you become more confident.

As a child you might have experienced cognitive dissonance on coming into contact with another child. If you believed it wasn't safe to be fully alive and expressive, because you were frequently admonished for "yahooing", "getting into things" and "being a nuisance", and someone came along intent on experimenting, exploring and talking a lot, you would have felt uneasy. To reduce your anxiety you might have justified your belief by telling yourself there was something wrong with that child; or you might have attempted to take control by getting the child to quieten down and stop "messing about" (thereby modelling your parents) so you no longer felt threatened. Alternatively, you could have changed your mind about aliveness and been more expressive yourself.

To sum up: cognitive dissonance is created when our beliefs are confronted.

> It is hardly any wonder that parents – still mainly tied to the industrial-era code book – find themselves in conflict with children who, aware of the growing irrelevance of the old rules, are uncertain, if not blindly ignorant, of the new ones
>
> Alvin Toffler

If a child associates pain with intuitively expressing aliveness, that person may still do so as an adult, albeit unconsciously. A child's unrestrained life urge may threaten a parent's limited belief systems. This creates anxiety in the parent, which he or she is then motivated to reduce. Imposing discipline or punishment on the child is, in many cases, the chosen means of doing this. Parents can, by suppressing a child's aliveness, spontaneity and natural expressiveness, reduce their own anxiety. Hence it is often the parents' drive to avoid anxiety that motivates them to shape their children's behaviour. This is true even in the case of a parents' wish for a child to do well at school. If, for example, the child fails an exam, this could produce a variety of parental anxieties —

fear of a detrimental effect on the status of the family, concern that the child will become a delinquent, or worry that the child will remain financially dependent overly long, to name but a few. Unfortunately the use of punishment has in the past been an easy choice to make. One reason for this is that punishment does work in modifying behaviour, although the detrimental long-term effect on a child can be devastating. Another reason is that punishment has been, and still is, culturally acceptable and encouraged. It isn't that long ago that intuitively expressive and independently thinking young people, especially women, were being committed to mental asylums as a form of control.

How can otherwise kind, gentle, sensitive parents treat their children in a cruel way? I have never met a parent who did not feel some anxiety or cognitive dissonance when punishing a child; the guilty parents' club is probably the largest unorganised club in the world. To treat a child cruelly, therefore, parents must find a way to justify their behaviour. Hence they vindicate themselves with statements such as, "It's for your own good", "This hurts me more than it hurts you" and "I'm doing it because I love you." Responses of this nature can form a family pattern which is repeated through the generations.

Parents with low self-esteem may find the only area of their lives in which they can experience a sense of control is with their children. Their frustration and anger at feeling out of control — either in some specific respect, e.g. at work, or in life more generally — is all too often taken out on their children. Such parents are not about to let an expressive and experimental kid get the better of them.

> If there is anything that we wish to change in the child, we should first examine it and see if it is not something that could better be changed in ourselves
>
> Carl Jung

45

Matters are complicated when parents respond differently on separate occasions to the same behaviour, depending on how they feel at the time. It is common for parents to punish and withdraw affection more often and with less provocation when they are stressed, anxious, unhappy, angry or dissatisfied over their own lives. If children have a clear idea of what is punishable, they know what behaviour to avoid. If they know the rules their parents are playing by, they can relax in the certainty that if they abide by those rules they will avoid pain and even receive approval. If, however, the rules keep changing, they will be unsure what behaviour will lead to pain. This creates apprehension, uncertainty and anxiety in children, causing them to hold back, reluctant to take the risk of asserting themselves.

Sometimes what strikes a child as parental inconsistency is caused by changes in circumstances of which he or she isn't aware. One day, playing with the hose in the garden is a fun experience that attracts no disapproval. The next day, with washing drying, the same activity leads to punishment. Digging in the garden is fine in the morning but becomes a punishable offence in the afternoon after seedlings have been planted. Helping Dad paint the bedroom wall is a pleasurable experience but becomes a punishable offence when undertaken a week later with one's own set of paints. All these activities — watering, digging, painting — are performed by parents; by engaging in them children are modelling their parents. If the error of their ways in such situations isn't explained to children in a loving way — if, instead, their parents' response is an angry outburst — they become confused and can shy away from expressing themselves in future. From experiences of this kind, children learn that they are unable to trust their judgement and choice of behaviour: it may be an okay choice, but then again it may not.

It is important that children's expressive energy, if inappropriately expressed, is redirected rather than suppressed; they need to be shown an appropriate way to express themselves so that they understand it isn't their expression in general that is at fault, only the specific instance.

If you hold beliefs that create anxiety, there is a good chance that your drive to avoid pain is causing you to push them out of your awareness. Do you imagine the rats in the experiment wanted to spend their days thinking about white boxes? Of course not. After the question was put to 73 rats the answer came back loud and clear: "Don't even think about white boxes." Who can blame them? Would you want to contemplate something if to do so reminded you of pain? Our drive to avoid pain motivates us to avoid thoughts that create anxiety. If thinking certain thoughts makes us feel anxious and fearful, we can reduce the anxiety and fear by repressing those thoughts. Repression is a function of our drive to avoid pain. It is the avoidance of anxiety-producing thoughts by pushing them out of our conscious awareness.

There are three major problems with repression as a strategy for avoiding pain. The first is that it doesn't remove the cause of anxiety; it just dampens down the effect by keeping the offending stimulus "out of sight", where it continues to have a disempowering impact. The second problem is the considerable effort it takes to be constantly unaware of something. It isn't one specific thing we link pain to, rather a whole network of thoughts, emotions and behaviour, and trying to keep them all repressed is a full-time job that can literally drain a person's energy, causing constant fatigue. The third problem is that repression cannot be confined to those things we decide are "bad". Since what we are repressing is our aliveness, all our aliveness is affected. Life becomes dull across the board. The more you repress, the closer you are to death.

## The drive to pursue pleasure

Working alongside the drive to avoid pain is the drive to pursue pleasure. This is another powerful motivator of behaviour. Our lives revolve around avoiding pain and seeking pleasure. On the pleasure side we want to feel happy and satisfied, and that we are loved and wanted. While avoiding pain, we also do what we believe will bring us these feelings.

We work because of the satisfaction it gives us, or because we enjoy what the money we earn buys us. We engage in relationships because giving and receiving love, experiencing companionship and having someone to share the journey of life with gives us pleasure. We choose activities and hobbies for the interest and fun we get out of them. We buy clothes that make us look good, which in turn makes us feel good. We choose the food we eat for the pleasure it gives us, the pleasure of taste and texture and of its beneficial effect on our health.

In conversation, too, we are motivated to pursue pleasure. We will steer a conversation in a particular direction to stimulate the encouragement and interest of those with whom we are talking. By nodding, making appropriate facial expressions and saying things like, "Is that right?", "Hey, that's interesting", "Wow, that's amazing", we can guide a conversation in the direction we want it to take. When we encourage someone in this way, they experience pleasure and modify their behaviour, in this case the way they speak, to get the maximum amount of pleasure. Try this out yourself and don't be surprised if the person you are conversing with gets very animated.

## Linking pain and pleasure: how we get our wires crossed

Having high self-esteem and the confidence to express ourselves is dependent on our life urge being encouraged and guided in ways that empower us. We express our life urge through our natural drives to explore, express and expand. When we are children, these natural drives are strong. We are full of energy and want to express it. It is often when we are exploring, experimenting and having fun that we get into trouble — for example, for pulling the pots out of the cupboard, pouring paint all over the floor, digging in the garden, spraying water with the garden hose, running around in an excited state, using a full bottle of shampoo in one go, drawing on the walls, spreading cat food across the floor, unrolling the toilet paper and pulling it round the house, or reaching out to touch and hold things on the supermarket shelves. How often, when you are shopping, do you hear children being told, "Don't touch that" or, "You'll get a smack if you do that once more"?

Exploration need not be this overt to meet with abusive behaviour. Simply asking questions is often met with an abusive response, as is putting forward ideas. Does the response "Don't be so stupid" sound familiar?

You can encounter parents using abusive behaviour towards their children everywhere you turn; you don't need to go in search of it. The result is that we learn to link pain to behaviour that is pleasurable, a process that continues throughout childhood.

> We do not need to be told whether to be strict or permissive with our children. What we do need is to have respect for their needs, feelings, and their individuality, as well as for our own
>
> Alice Miller

It isn't just at home or with parents that this conditioning takes place. School is another formative environment. I remember a time at college when my class had a particularly poor maths teacher. He would have the day's lesson written up on the board when the class arrived, and once everyone was seated — without any explanation of what we were to do — he would say, "There it is. Are there any questions?" On our very first day with this teacher a number of us raised our hands, but that was to be the last time. This man was a master at inflicting pain. Picking out a boy who had raised his hand, he asked, "What is it you don't understand?", but before the boy could respond he continued with, "Is there something wrong with you? Everyone else in the class understands." Well, any hands that were still in the air went down lightning fast; the kid was on his own. No-one else was going to admit ignorance in the face of such a challenge.

How would a child feel in this situation? I can tell you — because I was that kid. Do you think I was in pain? I was in *massive* pain. I felt as if I had failed before I had even started, as well as humiliated and embarrassed in front of my friends. Enough pain was applied in those few moments to ensure that not only did I never ask a question in that class ever again but nor did anyone else. We were simply too unwilling to take the risk; not knowing what we were meant to be doing seemed less irksome than speaking up. Our class bottomed out that year with the lowest grades in the school, and I'm quite sure most of the class ended up with deeply negative associations around the subject of maths in particular and asking for help and understanding in general — I certainly did.

This incident demonstrates the conditioning process in which behaviour in one situation can be linked to pain in such a way that contemplation of similar behaviour in another situation signals the likelihood of unpleasant consequences. I couldn't repress the thought of school entirely to lessen the pain, but I did manage to be absent on enough days for it to be suggested I might be wasting my time there; on reflection I'm sure I was.

## *Fear: a conditioned response*

As well as demonstrating the way in which we learn to link pain with the desire for pleasure (or satisfaction of some kind), the example above also illustrates the conditioned nature of fear. Here is another example.

In 1920, pioneer behaviourist John Watson set out to prove that most fears are learnt by conditioning an 11-month-old baby called Albert to fear white laboratory rats. Watson found he could cause Albert to experience anxiety with the sound produced by striking a steel bar with a hammer. Albert was presented with a white rat, and the moment his curiosity motivated him to reach out and touch it, the bar was struck, scaring him. (You may wonder at the humanity of this method of proving a point.) With each successive repetition of this exercise the more disturbed Albert became, until just the sight of the white rat caused him to cry. But Albert's new conditioned fear did not remain confined to rats; it became generalised to other animals or objects that shared similarities with a rat. On seeing a fur coat, dog or rabbit Albert would also burst into tears.

*All* the components of a situation in which we experience pain can become linked to pain. If we are experiencing pleasure when the pain occurs, pleasure becomes linked to pain; if we are feeling excited, excitement becomes linked to pain; if we are being expressive, self-expression becomes linked; if we are enjoying our body, that becomes linked. If raising a hand with the intention of asking a question draws the response of being put down and humiliated in front of the class, the pain of this experience can become linked to hand-raising, question-asking, teachers, the classroom and school as a whole.

We modify our behaviour in order to avoid a situation and the pain that we have come to associate with it. We will avoid love, sex, intimacy and aliveness in all its forms if they have become linked to pain. In other words, we adapt. Albert avoided white rats and similar animals or objects. I refrained from raising my hand and asking questions for years; in fact, just raising my hands above my head in *any* situation, even at play, created anxiety until I purposely changed my associations. Through association our mind concludes that the pleasurable feeling of excitement, say, is also responsible for the painful experience of punishment. Our belief then becomes, "If I want to avoid being punished, I have to avoid getting excited." We avoid getting excited by refraining from doing anything that would make us feel that way. Avoid excitement and we avoid punishment; avoid pleasure and we avoid pain.

## *Are you pursuing pleasure or avoiding pain?*

Whatever you focus on will expand. If you focus on pleasure, you will experience more pleasure. If you focus on pain, you will find more pain. *Your mind will seek out whatever you direct it to look upon.* We all have pain we want to move away from, and that's fine. However, if during childhood your primary focus was trying to move away from pain, you may still be doing the same thing as an adult, which will invariably create more pain for yourself. Is your main focus on trying to escape from where you *don't* want to be, or is it on moving towards where you *do* want to be?

On first consideration there may not seem to be much difference between these two attitudes, but there is a world of difference in the results they create. If you focus on pain, albeit on moving away from it, you will tend to carry that pain forward with you. Your mind will move you towards whatever you focus on. By the same token, if you focus on something you want, your mind will move you towards that. The key to instantly transforming the quality of your life is to take your focus off pain and place it on pleasure.

Take, for example, a person who chooses to move from the city to live in the country. There could be disadvantages in such a move — a lack of evening entertainment, a minimal social life and few shops, for instance. However, if the person has decided to make the move because of the value he places on nature, peace and a slow pace of life — if he is positively seeking these things — he will dismiss any qualms about what he is giving up.

> To do something because the psychological consequences of not doing it are too painful is quite different from doing something because of the gratification it provides.
>
> Alfie Kohn

Another person could decide to make the same move but for a very different reason — for example, to distance himself from a broken relationship. His focus — i.e. his motivation for moving — is what he *doesn't* want, and what he *does* want isn't taken into consideration. He has a goal of sorts — less pain — but because he isn't intent on actively achieving or enjoying something, on thriving in a supportive environment, his mind is actually still focused on his pain, which he will therefore carry with him.

Start moving towards what you do want by asking yourself empowering questions. Instead of asking, "How can I stop feeling guilty?" ask, "What can I do to experience innocence?" Instead of asking, "How can I get rid of this fear?" ask, "What can I do that will make me feel confident?"

# 6

## The beliefs that destroy confidence

### From pain to pleasure

CONFIDENCE comes from trusting one's actions will lead to an experience of pleasure. When we lack confidence it is because we are unsure of our ability to avoid pain of some kind. When we describe ourselves as "not confident", we are expressing an expectation of pain. "I'm not confident enough to do that" is really saying, "I might fail", "I might do it wrong", "I might be rejected" or "I don't know enough to succeed." Such statements are expressions of an expectation of pain. When we lack confidence it is because we have associated pain with whatever we are contemplating doing.

Our parents shape the way we think and behave by teaching us to link pain to certain kinds of behaviour (from which we then refrain) and pleasure to others, depending on what is and isn't okay with them. During the conditioning process we form conclusions about the experience; these conclusions we adopt as disempowering beliefs, e.g. "I must do as I'm told." It is important to be aware, however, that even though our parents provide the stimulus that shapes our behaviour, it is *our own thoughts* about the stimulus that determine what our behaviour will be. We always *choose* what we consider the *best response* to any situation in which we find ourselves. We form beliefs about the best strategies for survival and base our behaviour on these. If, when you were a child, not speaking up worked well for you — in other words, if it enabled you to avoid discomfort — you will have decided it was a good strategy, and unless a situation subsequently arises which prompts you to decide otherwise, you will employ that strategy for the rest of your life. If misbehaving proved to be the only way of getting attention when you wanted it, you will have adopted that as a strategy. If being "good" or doing what you were told seemed to be an effective means of avoiding pain and getting what you wanted, you will have adopted that approach. Behaviour that proves successful in avoiding pain or guaranteeing pleasure becomes firmly implanted in our minds as the preferred strategy. We believe in it because it works. This is the essence of conditioning.

After a time we become unaware that we are operating by these beliefs; they become subconscious. We have mastered low self-esteem and don't even know it. This conditioning can stay with us into adulthood, and through the repeated cycle of children modelling their parents, family patterns of behaviour are perpetuated from generation to generation.

The drive to avoid pain creates a lack of confidence. Or, to put it in reverse, to have no confidence is a good strategy for avoiding pain. Once you have linked enough pain to taking action, you can kiss goodbye to confidence.

 *Because you recognise your own uniqueness you will not need to dominate others, nor cringe before them*

Jane Roberts

If you believed that any action you took would increase your experience of pleasure, would you lack confidence? If you knew that every mistake you made was considered a natural part of the learning process, that drew no disapproval and no disempowering judgements, wouldn't you experience greater confidence? And what if you knew you would receive all the support and encouragement you could possibly need to succeed — wouldn't that make you feel confident? And if

55

you received all this encouragement for doing what you wanted to do, based on your own intuition and curiosity, do you think you would be motivated to make your dreams a reality? Just imagine what you could achieve with this kind of encouragement.

## Unblock the flow of confidence

There are a number of specific beliefs that commonly block confidence and self-esteem. If these are challenged and re-placed with alternative, empowering beliefs, the way is opened to express one's true self.

### Disempowering belief 1

#### PLEASURE LEADS TO PAIN

Aiming for what we want and expressing our aliveness are pleasurable experiences. However, if they consistently lead to a painful experience, we learn to anticipate pain whenever we experience pleasure. It is a small, logical step from that to realising we can avoid pain by avoiding pleasure — or get-ting "overexcited", as our parents may have called it. ("Overexcitement" is a term used by people with a low toler-ance for pleasure.)

We betray our belief that pleasure leads to pain whenever we make statements such as, "It can't last", "It's too good to be true", "If it gets any better I'll die." Using language of this kind sends a powerful message to the brain — that things had better not get any better! It makes a major association between pain and pleasure. How about this for an expec-tation of pain: "You'd better have fun now before it's too late"?

A few years ago I had an interesting experience that dem-onstrated to me the power of the belief that pleasure leads to pain. A friend was giving me a massage. It was a beautiful day and we were in a beautiful setting. Relaxing music soothed my mind as the tension flowed from my body. By the end of the massage I was on cloud nine and feeling totally relaxed. I was hosting a barbecue that afternoon and had to take the gas bottle for a refill. As I was driving down the road feeling great, I realised I was also feeling guilty. My mind was saying, "You shouldn't feel this good", and then the thought popped up, "How can I get some stress back in my life?" If you ask a question you invariably get an answer. My answer just walked out in front of the car in the form of a man leading his whole family onto the road without bothering to look to see if there was anything coming. Stress was now happening big time. Fortunately I missed them, but I was forced to hit the brakes so hard that the gas bottle came flying forward, bounced off the back of the seat and shot through the rear window. Boy, was I mad. I got out and yelled and screamed — and the damage was done. It didn't help to find out that the family came from a little town in the South Island where they didn't have to think about traffic. In fact, regardless of their part in this little drama, I am sure I was subconsciously on the lookout for a situation to prove to myself that pleasure leads to pain. With a belief like this, one can never underestimate how creative our minds can be at finding ways to sabotage pleasure.

Until the belief that pleasure leads to pain is challenged, the cycle of adverse conditioning, with its damaging consequences for confidence, will continue. To break the cycle, turn the process of conditioning in the opposite direction and bolster confidence, the first belief to adopt is:

PLEASURE ALWAYS LEADS TO MORE PLEASURE

This can be reinforced by the following:

• It's safe to be outrageous
• Being outrageous is good for me
• Going for it is safe and pleasurable
• I deserve pleasure

## *Disempowering belief 2*

### I HAVE TO CONTROL MYSELF
### IT ISN'T SAFE TO BE FULLY ALIVE

If, as children, we get "carried away" with the joy of exploring and expressing ourselves, we all too often incur the unpleasantness of our parents' disapproval. We learn to think we are doing something wrong when we behave in this way, and come to expect to be admonished. In this situation we adopt a strategy of self-control. We learn that if we control our aliveness and keep our energy output at an "acceptable" level, we will avoid the pain of disapproval and receive the balm of approval instead.

You may recall fun times being interrupted like this: "Stop that! You've been having too much of a good time. Now settle down" — which meant, control your level of excitement or you're in trouble. Parents can of course be more direct still, with threats such as, "Control yourself or you're going straight to bed", or, worse, "Control yourself or you'll get a good hiding." (I have often wondered if "good" in this context means "thorough" or if its use is intended to imply beatings are good and the child bad.) Some parents even say, "I'll kill you if you do that."

Not only is having fun a punishable offence. Children can be punished for being upset, too, instead of being given sympathy and understanding. Tears can earn a blow or confinement in a bedroom. We quickly learn to suppress or hide a whole range of emotions.

It is only a small step from here to concluding that it simply isn't safe to be fully alive (a "truth" first borne upon us while making that epic transition from the womb into the world).

In what ways are you controlling yourself? How often do you hold back your aliveness? Do you suppress your emotions? What sort of an effect do you think controlling your energy levels is having on your life? In what ways is it affecting your health and relationships? Are you secretly afraid that, if you let others know how you really feel, they will reject you or not want to know you any more? Do you "play it safe" at work, believing that if you're too "different" or "off-beat" your work mates won't want to know you or you'll lose your job? What impact is holding back your aliveness having on your ability to give? Do you think you can give effectively to others if you aren't willing to give yourself an experience of aliveness?

The degree to which we suppress our aliveness is reflected in our level of commitment. When we hold back a part of ourselves, we aren't fully present. Our relationships are less than they could be; the sparks don't fly as they might; adventure is limited. For a truly great relationship, both parties need to be committed to being ever more fully present and fully alive. If you fear expressing yourself fully in your relationships, you may justify holding back by saying, "My partner can't handle my aliveness", or "I'm too much." It is more likely, however, that your partner would love to experience more of your aliveness, and to respond by expressing more of his or her own.

Life is an experience of energy, and if that energy is suppressed every area of life is detrimentally affected. Hence, the second belief to adopt in the pursuit of confidence is:

IT'S SAFE TO BE FULLY ALIVE

This can be reinforced by the following:

• The more freely I express myself, the more I get what I want
  • I can easily handle being fully alive
  • My aliveness is a source of pleasure for myself and others
  • I forgive myself for holding back

## *Disempowering belief 3*
### I'M GUILTY

Our parents blame us for the pain they inflict on us. If they withdraw their love, it's our fault. If we get a smack, we asked for it. We receive the message time and again: "You're bad. Behave yourself." We are reprimanded and affection is withdrawn, and it is our behaviour that has caused this. It is not by chance that in the back of our mind there lurk thoughts such as, "I'm bad", "It's all my fault", "I'm not good enough", "I'm wrong" and "I'm to blame" — thoughts to which we are usually unwilling to admit. If we are consistently told off and judged "bad", we come to believe the judgement. A child's mind needs a reason why a supposedly loving parent should inflict pain — personal "badness" and "guilt" seem like good reasons. By taking the blame we can justify our parents' abusive actions.

We do not confine this judgement of ourselves to the behaviour that draws parental criticism; we assume the thoughts and feelings that motivated us to behave in the way we did are also at fault. Because it is the natural and spontaneous self-expression that wells up from inside us that is being judged, we conclude we are essentially "no good" at our core.

The third belief to adopt in order to experience self-confidence, therefore, is:

I'M INNOCENT

This can be reinforced by the following beliefs:

- I'm not responsible for other people's feelings
- I'm more than good enough
- My self-expression is innocent
- I'm all right

*Disempowering belief 4*

I'M STUPID
I'M INCOMPETENT

If, in childhood, you experienced a lack of encouragement, or your opinions were put down or ridiculed with statements such as, "Don't be stupid", "Don't be so ridiculous" or "That's a silly idea", the beliefs about you such censure illustrates may be operating in your own subconscious mind. If, while you were following your intuition and developing your mental skills of reasoning, your parents constantly devalued, brushed aside or overrode your ideas, the powerful disempowering effect this would have had may still be affecting you in your adulthood.

> We may soon discover that all babies are born geniuses and only become degeniused by the erosive effects of unthinkingly maintained false assumptions of the grown-ups, with their conventional ways of "bringing up" and "educating" their young.
>
> R. Buckminster Fuller

We learn not to trust our own thoughts and feelings, and to have no confidence in our actions. The expectation of pain, whether in the form of punishment or failure, is enough to prompt us to sit back and await instructions. If we don't believe our ideas are good enough and we don't want to make painful "mistakes" by "getting it wrong", we develop a reluctance to initiate things. We suppress our creative urge. Subsequently, in adulthood, we project our belief in our inadequacy by putting down other people's thoughts and ideas. How often have you heard conversations in which statements such as this are used: "That'll never work", "You can't do that", "You must be dreaming", "What you're thinking of is impossible" and "Don't be an idiot"? If you find yourself judging others, check your own beliefs — you may be projecting.

The fourth belief to adopt in order to experience confidence is:

I AM IMPORTANT AND MY IDEAS ARE VALUABLE

This can be reinforced by the following:

- I'm intelligent
- I have confidence in my ideas
- What I offer is of value

## *Disempowering belief 5*

### I'M SAFE WHEN I'M OUT OF SIGHT
### I HAVE MORE FREEDOM IF I'M NOT SEEN

This is a strategy for avoiding pain by avoiding the pain-giver. When we are alone or out of sight of our parents, we have greater freedom to express ourselves. We can get on undisturbed with doing our own thing and be more adventurous. By learning to be invisible we can create our own comfortable little world in which we feel safe. This hiding strategy can become a way of life in adulthood, with damaging consequences. Can you imagine running a business with such an approach to life? Success usually depends on being visible, be the venture in question writing a book, running a cafe or selling a product. If you can't be seen by your customer you may as well not exist, because to the customer you don't.

We may extend this hiding strategy to embrace all our thoughts and feelings, wishes and desires, in order to keep them secret and out of harm's way. This is where they then stay, locked away inside us. Our feelings in particular can get a severe battering when we are young, and not letting them show allows us to retain some sense of ourselves.

The fifth belief to adopt in order to experience confidence is:

### IT'S SAFE AND PLEASURABLE TO BE SEEN

This can be reinforced by the following:

- Being "out there" is immensely pleasurable
- When I'm visible, I prosper
- I freely and safely express myself
- Sharing my thoughts and feelings gives me pleasure
- When people see me, they see my innocence

## *Disempowering belief 6*
### LOVE IS PAINFUL

Why do we put up with so much abuse from other people, and why is it that some of the worst abuse can come from friends and loved ones? We are conditioned to believe that being punished or abused is actually good for us, and that the abusers either love us or are looking out for our well-being. When punishment is perceived as "for our own good", to keep us in line or to prepare us for life, we conclude that "I need to be disciplined" and "Pain is good for me." "Show me you love me" becomes an invitation to abuse. We buy the lines "I'm doing it because I love you" and "This hurts me more than it hurts you." Our parents love us so much that they are apparently willing to inflict pain on themselves to try to get us to behave in a certain way.

We have a strong bond of love with our parents, a bond that is formed in our mother's womb and reinforced when we feed at her breast. Our mother and father are our protectors, and we are totally dependent on them. From them we learn how to survive in the world; the example they set is our model. When parents abuse their children in subtle and not so subtle ways, this bond of love becomes contaminated with pain. When the parents we love cause us pain, we learn to expect pain from those we love; it can even become a prerequisite for the experience of love. If someone is not causing us pain of some description, we can doubt they actually love us; after all, our mind reasons, our parents loved us and they caused us pain. Some people will leave a relationship because their partner is too nice. The partner treats them well, which isn't the way they were used to being treated as a child, so they leave to find a person who will treat them abusively.

The sixth belief to adopt in order to experience confidence is:

**LOVE IS KINDNESS, GENTLENESS, ENCOURAGEMENT AND SUPPORT — I DESERVE LOVE**

This can be reinforced by the following:

- I'm the best judge of what is good for me
- There's only room for loving people in my life
- Abuse is abuse, love is love

# 7

## *Conditioned to conform: the authority problem*

*I*F, during childhood, we internalised the disempowering beliefs discussed in the previous chapter, we will lack self-confidence. Without self-confidence, we will experience anxiety whenever we are faced with making a decision. We can avoid this anxiety by not making any decisions, by ignoring our own preferences and leaving it to others to determine what we should or should not do. In other words, we can conform to the will of others. Loss of confidence is a prerequisite for conforming.

Once we have lost confidence in ourselves and our ability to avoid pain, we have a "need" (although we may not want to admit it) for someone to take care of us — to make sure we don't get into trouble, to give us the nourishment and money we require, and to provide us with the direction we think is necessary to guide us through what seems to be a scary, pain-filled world. (It is interesting to note that these are the very needs the prison system fulfils.) During our child-hood our parents fill this role; they are the principal authority in our lives, and on the whole most of us conform to their wishes, even though in some cases we may be, or feel, forced to do so and resent it.

When the time comes for us to step out into the world on our own, we must give up the security upon which we have become dependent; yet we have now been conditioned to need an authority in our lives, so we search out replacements for our parents. We can transfer their responsibility onto anyone who presents themselves as an authority, or anyone who we perceive as an authority. This means that the dynamics of our relationship with authority, established within our relationship with our parents, can be transferred to teachers, employers, gurus, doctors, accountants, politicians, experts, landlords, businesses, banks, the media, corporations, the police, the prison system or government departments — to name but a few. We get a job and confer on our employer the role of parent. Our employer provides us with money, tells us what to do and disapproves if we don't "perform", i.e. if we are "bad". We enter into a relationship in which we expect our employer to look after us and to give us the love and approval that we haven't learnt to give ourselves — something an employer cannot do.

If we weren't given the opportunity to experience equality of worth with our parents, we won't have learnt to communicate equally with those who represent authority — we will relate to them as if they are superior, if we have the courage to approach them at all. Our communication will be coloured by all the unresolved emotion of our past. This is demonstrated by the violence, resentment, blame and anger, both overt and covert, that so many people direct towards authorities of all kinds.

One measure of the extent to which you conform is the amount of risk you habitually take. Another is the degree of creativity you express. Risk-taking and creativity are both anticonformist by nature, and as such can draw disapproval. Avoiding any action that might draw disapproval suppresses creativity. (In fact, risk-taking is but one expression of creativity.)

> *A man must consider what a rich realm he abdicates when he becomes a conformist.*
> Ralph Waldo Emerson

If you are taking risks that could arouse the disapproval of others, you are on the track to non-conformity and loosening the ties of authority. If you are being innovative, it is highly likely that at first you will meet with resistance. Many people are so afraid of change that they strongly resist new ideas and defend old ideas most forcefully, as if their survival depends on it — which, in fact, they believe it does. Such behaviour is an indication of low self-esteem and conditioned conformity.

## *The comfort of conformity*

By waiting for and conforming to instruction and direction from others, we are able to worry less about making mistakes, and to an extent we avoid the threats and challenges of the world. We avoid having to address fears, anxieties and doubts associated with following our own intuitively chosen path. Conforming can in fact be quite comfortable, for it appears to offer a reasonable degree of security.

It is the comfort of conformity which represents the biggest obstacle to following our true selves. There seems to be a lot at stake when we consider choosing and following our own path. We fear disapproval and losing the love and support of those close to us; we fear jeopardising a consistent flow of income; we fear making wrong choices; we fear being seen as different and no longer belonging; we worry about being unable to make a living and support ourselves. With little faith in our intuition, creativity and personal power, and with undeveloped communication skills, we can feel poorly equipped to step out on our own. When the idea of following our heart and forging a unique life path creates so much anxiety, conforming can seem an attractive option even at the expense of missing out on the magic life has to offer. Although consciously we may say we want freedom and independence, so often we are afraid to pursue them. There is no doubt it takes courage to break free of conditioning and map out one's own life journey, but the joy and self-respect it brings are rewards well worth the effort. In fact, it is impossible to respect ourselves fully until we are following our own path. Following our own path *is* respecting ourselves.

67

# The language of disempowerment

Disempowering beliefs are betrayed by the language we habitually use. By continuing to employ some of the vocabulary first adopted during childhood, we keep ourselves trapped in powerlessness. The use of statements such as "I should...", "I'd better..." and "I ought to..." is often an indication of feelings of guilt and obligation. If you are using these, you may be disempowering yourself. Give yourself permission to do what you *want* to do, not what you think you *should* do. If you have obligations, make sure they are obligations you really want to have. Ask yourself, "Do I want to do this and is it important to me?" Tell the truth about it — "I want to do it" or "I don't want to do it." If you are giving out of guilt, you aren't doing yourself any good, nor those to whom you are giving; instead of promoting love, you are promoting resentment.

We use statements such as, "I might..." or "I could..." when we aren't sure whether it's okay to do something; we're testing the ground. If there are no objections, we might go ahead. In other words, we seek permission. Such statements reflect a fear of committing to what we want and a lack of self-trust. There's a big difference between "I might start work at ten this morning" and "I'm starting work at ten this morning." The first is really saying, "I might start work at ten but I don't want to create any pain for myself." Any attempt to create high self-esteem will be sabotaged by the continued use of disempowering language.

# Break the mould of conformity

In challenging the beliefs that trap us in conformity and replacing them with new, empowering beliefs, we learn to honour ourselves and free ourselves from an internalised need to be controlled. It is important to bear in mind, however, that to honour oneself in no way entails having a disrespect for others or invalidating others' needs. It certainly doesn't entail meeting one's own needs at the expense of others'. We all have obligations to other people and to society at large, at the forefront of which is the expansion of love and compassion. This means doing what we can to take the abuse, disrespect, prejudices and discriminations out of human relations. It means improving the ways in which we live, interact, run our businesses and care for our environment so as to ensure generations to come have a greater opportunity for a high quality of life. It *doesn't* mean selfishly doing one's own thing, without regard for the wellbeing of others.

We all share the same basic needs — for love, respect and an experience of aliveness. If we learn to meet the real needs of ourselves, we will better understand how to meet the real needs of others.

There are a number of specific beliefs that trap us into conforming. If these are challenged and replaced with alternative, empowering beliefs, the way is opened to express one's true self.

## *Disempowering belief 1*
### I MUST DO AS I'M TOLD

If you find yourself automatically complying with requests others make of you, even though you are thinking, "I don't want to do this", and feeling resentful as a consequence, you have been conditioned to do as you are told. As young children we quickly learn that when we do what we are told we usually receive our parents' approval, love, support, praise or acknowledgement — and sometimes a reward. We naturally conclude that doing what we are told is a good strategy for getting good feelings. The value of this strategy is further reinforced when we discover disobedience leads to bad feelings. Once these twin beliefs are internalised, we act on them without conscious awareness. Believing we must do as we are told — to feel good and avoid pain — we are motivated to look around for instructions to follow, causing us to set up our whole life under the direction of others.

This isn't the kind of belief that personal independence is built on. Look at your own life and ask yourself who's directing it. Are you making the decisions or are you giving someone else that power? If you want to experience true aliveness, you must be self-directed, hence the first belief to adopt in order to break the mould of conformity is:

### I LOOK TO MYSELF FOR DIRECTION

This can be reinforced by the following:

- I make up my own mind
- It's safe for me to think my own thoughts and take my own actions
- I trust my decisions and actions to bring me pleasure
- I can successfully guide myself to pleasure

## *Disempowering belief 2*
### QUESTIONING GETS ME INTO TROUBLE

It doesn't take long to discover the folly of questioning the "do what you are told" approach. We quickly learn that the requests and demands of our parents are generally not to be questioned if we want to avoid pain. It isn't long before we adopt the strategy of not asking questions, which involves the avoidance of speaking up, saying what we think or complaining when we think we're getting a raw deal.

We come to adopt this non-questioning strategy in relation to all forms of authority, automatically assuming that rules and policies must be followed. Anything written we consider gospel. What we see on TV and read in the newspapers we automatically take as the truth. Is it any wonder many of us play the role of victim? We have been well trained. In particular, we learn not to question "No". This word often becomes directly linked to massive pain, and we will do our utmost to avoid it. "No" is one of the most powerful fear-inducing words, yet it is only when we have placed the source of love outside ourselves that it has a disempowering effect.

The second belief to adopt in order to break the mould of conformity is:

QUESTIONING INCREASES MY POWER AND PLEASURE

This can be reinforced by the following:

- I'm free to question anything and everything
- I'm the authority in my life
- I'm deserving of respect
- I expect respect from others
- I'm loved and wanted
- I love and accept myself

## *Disempowering belief 3*
### I NEED PERMISSION

The two conforming strategies identified so far — to do as we're told, and not to question that — keep us secure. We soon learn a third — that we can express ourselves and do the things we want only if we have permission. We become conditioned to need permission to speak, act, do enjoyable things, venture out on our own and receive.

The need for permission is conveyed by commands such as, "Put that down", "Stop that", "Put that away", "Put that back", "Leave that alone" and "Don't touch that." Then there are warnings such as, "Do that again and..." or, "This is the last warning." All these responses to our behaviour can cause us to hold back until we receive permission. We are forced to ask, "Can I have...?" or, "Can I play with...?" We may be further forced into submission by having to say please, in effect being forced to plead for pleasure.

As the need for permission from someone other than ourselves becomes internalised and adopted as a strategy, we continue the handing over of power to someone else. We can waste a whole life waiting for permission to live it, permission that may never come. The third belief to adopt in order to break the mould of conformity, therefore, is:

71

## I GIVE MYSELF PERMISSION TO EXPLORE
## AND TRY NEW THINGS

This can de reinforced by the following:

- I'm my own authority
- I give myself permission to receive love
- I give myself permission to receive money
- I give myself permission to experience pleasure
- It's safe for me to communicate what I want
- When I do ask for permission, I remain empowered and true to myself

*If you fear making anyone mad, then you ultimately probe for the lowest common denominator of human achievement.*

Jimmy Carter

## *Disempowering belief 4*
### IF I PLEASE OTHERS, I CAN AVOID PAIN

This belief is the basis of martyrdom. To live by its dictates translates into attempting to get your needs met by being a "good" employee and a "good" citizen. "Good" means doing what you think you should be doing and not what you really want to be doing. "Good" isn't really good at all. If you attempt to meet your needs for acceptance, approval and love by rushing around helping others, you are doomed to end up frustrated, resentful and exhausted. This belief and the behaviour that springs from it involve self-violation.

The fourth belief to adopt in order to break the mould of conformity is:

## PEOPLE ENJOY MY PRESENCE MOST WHEN
## I'M BEING TRUE TO MYSELF

This can be reinforced by the following:

- I'm responsible for my own pleasure and pain
- I get what I want when I please myself
- Everyone benefits when I please myself
- To feel happy is a matter of personal choice for each individual

## *Disempowering belief 5*

### WHAT AN AUTHORITY WANTS IS MORE IMPORTANT THAN WHAT I WANT, THINK OR FEEL

If our parents ignore our ideas, dismiss our feelings, and give our needs and desires low priority, we conclude that what we want isn't important. We can end up feeling that our experience of life, or our view of how things are, isn't valid. We learn that our needs are secondary to the needs of our parents, and as adults continue to place others' needs before our own. Constant invalidation can easily lead to the conclusion that *we* aren't important or don't matter; not only do we devalue our wants, we devalue ourselves.

The fifth belief to adopt in order to break the mould of conformity is:

### I ENJOY MEETING MY OWN NEEDS

This can be reinforced by the following:

- My wants and needs are of utmost importance
- I'm important
- I've clearly defined the needs that are important to me

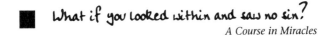

What if you looked within and saw no sin?

*A Course in Miracles*

## *Disempowering belief 6*

### TO GO FOR WHAT I WANT IS SELFISH

The world is bursting with people who won't admit to wanting anything for fear of being labelled selfish.

Selfishness can be defined as taking or receiving some-thing to someone else's detriment, i.e. one person's gain is another person's pain. An act is selfish if it entails someone missing out or being disadvantaged. The concept of selfish-ness derives in part from the notion of scarcity. We call others selfish when we believe they are taking from us, depleting what we possess or have access to. "Don't be selfish" is some-thing we often say when we fear there won't be enough for ourselves — in other words, when we are attempting to pro-tect our own interests. Our saying it then indicates we are just as concerned about scarcity and going without as the person we are labelling selfish.

Being selfish also implies an unwillingness to give to others, something people are likely to feel when they believe they don't have enough for themselves. They hold onto relation-ships because they think they'd be unable to find another partner. They hold onto money believing it will be hard to replace. When we hold onto things in this way, we are holding our limiting beliefs in place. Even when we are unwilling to give, we may still do so to avoid being thought selfish. Whenever this is our motivation for giving, we give with resentment. This is quite different from giving because we intuitively want to share. "Give and ye shall receive" is indeed accurate. Give with resentment and you will become more resentful and resented. Just as surely, give with love and you will become more loving and loved.

An unwillingness to give, giving with resentment, holding onto things, excessive acquisition of things and taking all one can — this is behaviour based on a disempowering belief in scarcity and lack.

To call going for what we want "selfish" and *not* going for what we want "good" or "correct" creates a hopeless situ-ation. If we go for what we want, we will feel all the guilt we associate with being selfish and this will destroy any joy we would otherwise get from our achievements. If we don't go for what we want, we make the decision that the guilt we would experience if we did would be more painful than miss-ing out. Once we have made this decision, we must suppress and deny our natural drives to explore, express and expand, thereby destroying any chance of experiencing joy in our lives. For some people, just the thought of having what they want arouses feelings of guilt sufficient to immobilise them.

Once we equate "having" with "selfish", we generalise the concept to all areas of our lives. Being happy, feeling good, experiencing pleasure, having a wonderful relationship, achieving a degree of wealth and being healthy can all be perceived as selfish. Hence, the sixth belief to adopt in order to break the mould of conformity is:

WHEN I GO FOR WHAT I WANT, I'M ENCOURAGING OTHERS TO GO FOR WHAT THEY WANT

This can be reinforced by:

- The more I have, the more I can give
- There's plenty for everyone
- I have the right to express myself freely
- In my quest for greater self-expression I easily move beyond old feelings of guilt and anxiety

## *Scarcity and competition*

Most of the disempowering beliefs discussed above are characterised by the notion of scarcity and lack. We believe we lack power and choice. We believe resources, money, time and love are all scarce. This culminates in an overall sense of being unable to get what we want out of life.

It isn't much of a step from the perception of scarcity to the conclusion that it is necessary to compete. Selfishness is competitive. Believing there isn't enough to go round we think it necessary to compete in order to get what we want. How aggressively we compete, or how selfishly we behave, depends on the extent to which we believe the scarcity we perceive threatens our survival. As soon as we perceive scarcity we adopt a win–lose mentality. In our relationships we want to have our own way, even if in subtle and secretive ways. At

75

work we might think of ourselves as on the lose side of the equation and our employer on the win side, so we "take what we can get" and give as little as we can get away with in return. Businesses operate on the premise that they have to compete for limited customers, limited money and limited resources, which causes them to proceed at the expense of the environment, their employees or other businesses with a share of the market. For a win–win outcome, we must all believe there is plenty for everyone.

If we have contaminated the idea of going for what we want with guilt, greed, competition and the notion of scarcity, our emotional energy and our behaviour will reflect these things. We will find ourselves disempowered and behaving in less than loving ways towards others and ourselves. When we function in this way, we are likely to accept what we don't want or at best only part of what we do want.

*You can get what you want in life.* You have the power and ability to meet your needs — by developing high self-esteem and a respect for others, and recognising that you are responsible for your own pleasure and pain. By altering your outlook and approach in this way, you will place yourself in a position to reach for your dreams. You will break out of the scarcity consciousness that is otherwise reinforced all around you and see that there is no lack of that which you truly want and need.

The next section of the book introduces the steps to follow and techniques to employ to bring effective change to your life and thus claim back your power.

# Part III

# *Embracing change*

# 8

## *Claim back your power and independence*

*A* number of years ago I became aware that I held the belief that I wasn't loved or wanted. Even though there were people in my life who did in fact love me, harbouring this belief meant I was unable to let the love in. I had just left a ten-year relationship which had started when I was eighteen, so all my self-doubts were coming to the fore.

It took me a while before I was willing to admit the belief to myself, and longer still before I could admit it to anyone else. I had been doing a good job of repressing it, so horrible a conviction did it appear. Holding it had prompted a strong emotional response and made me want to withdraw. When my relationship ended, I felt as if I had entered a world of women I didn't understand and feared. At the same time I felt I needed to learn what it meant to be a man. I also wanted to attract a new relationship, but not just any relationship — I wanted someone special.

I therefore had a number of very good reasons to change my beliefs, and I wanted to change fast. I was willing to focus all my resources on making the change, and soon realised that, as a first step, I was going to have to take full responsibility for my thinking and my life if I was going to be effective. Other steps were to follow.

# *Take responsibility for your life*

The moment you take responsibility for the present state of your life, you also claim the power to change it. You aren't responsible for the conditioning you received during childhood, but you must take responsibility for the life you have built as a result if you want to create something different.

 *Liberty means responsibility. That is why most men dread it*

George Bernard Shaw

If things are going to change for you, you have to change. You cannot alter your circumstances if you deny having had any part in their creation. The jilted lover who says, "I'm not responsible for my partner leaving; it had nothing to do with me", obviously won't even start to look for clues to why the relationship ended within him- or herself. Such a person will go on to the next relationship only to find after a period of time that the new partner leaves also. A person who attracts the same type of partner over and over again, and then concludes that all men or women are the same, is hardly taking responsibility. Taking responsibility for what is happening in your life frees up your creative power. You are then in a position to make the changes you want.

## *Give up resentment and blame*

There is no more effective way of keeping yourself bound to the past than to resent and blame your parents (or anyone else for that matter). Resenting and blaming can become conditioned mental habits. Blaming others for your problems may appear to help you avoid your own pain and to feel better about yourself — for example, you can dodge some of the pain associated with self-responsibility — but the problem with this is that as long as you blame and resent others, your mind will continue to search for pain in your life to justify the blaming and resenting.

> Clearing your past enables you to truly
> release guilt and blame, to truly forgive
> yourself and others, and to feel really good
> about yourself and your whole life
>
> Pamela Whitney

If your mind cannot find any pain, it will create some. Blaming and resenting stem from the assumption that what is desired but cannot be had is made unavailable by a party beyond one's control, be it another person, the government or life itself. When we disown our personal creative power, we shift responsibility for our circumstances and experience onto something or someone else. We then see ourselves as victims at the mercy of that outside party.

When you take responsibility for your thoughts and beliefs, you put yourself in the driving seat of your creative power and can choose in which direction you will head. You can remove limiting beliefs and adopt liberating alternatives, which will enable you to experience greater freedom. You can start creating your ideal experience of life — loving relationships, fulfilling work, supportive environments, good health, all-round vitality, and abundance of whatever else it is you want. You become the true authority in your life.

## *Choose your own beliefs*

If you commit to doing your own thinking, you can base your life on beliefs from which you want to operate rather than disempowering conditioned beliefs. You can learn to choose how you think by using your own intuition. Trust yourself — you can make good choices. You are the only person who knows what you want to create and how you want to lead your life. Are your current beliefs guiding you towards a destiny you don't want? Choose a path you *do* want and create a life in harmony with your true beliefs and values. Don't go along with others because of peer-group, social or cultural pressure. Ignore those that say, "You can't think that" or, "You can't do that." Thinking for oneself isn't always a popular activity, but if you make a private pact to think for yourself — to follow your natural curiosity and let your drive to explore guide your choices — you will open the way to the rewards of self-fulfilment.

■ To find yourself, think for yourself

Socrates

Most people want others to think as they do, to hold the same beliefs and values, leaving no room for individuality. It isn't usually that they are happy or successful and want others to share their joy; more often than not it is a sense of insecurity that motivates them to defend their own beliefs by attacking those of others. Only an insecure position needs defending; a secure one will stand on its own. Would you rather be right or happy?

It is easy to accept the opinions of others on the assumption that they must be better informed than oneself. It is far wiser, however — not to mention safer — to assume nothing of the sort. When a number of people get together out of a sense of insecurity and a need to have their ideas validated, a potentially dangerous situation arises. Many conflicts are started this way, and some religious groups are the worst offenders.

Businesses try to influence us through advertising. TV and other media continually bombard us with messages telling us what we should look like, what we should wear, what we should eat, what we should drive — and on it goes. Advertising can be very persuasive. Corporations pay millions of dollars for the most effective ways of influencing our behaviour. Repetition is a powerful tool.

We can become so detached from our essence that we lose touch with our own beliefs, values and ideals. Thinking for oneself may not be the easiest road to take, but it is the road that leads to the greatest rewards. Question your personal, family and cultural beliefs. This is the vital next step, after taking responsibility for your current situation, in taking control of your own destiny.

### Link pleasure to doing your own thinking

You can condition yourself to do your own thinking by using the same conditioning process that shaped you during childhood. You can link pleasure to behaviour you want to adopt — in this case, thinking for yourself — and pain to behaviour you want to avoid — doing as you're told against your wishes.

**Step 1** *Associate pain with doing what you are told.* Imagine yourself doing something you don't want to do, such as going to a job you don't like. Create a mental picture of yourself not achieving what you want in life because of having to do this thing. Imagine the long-term effect of continuing down this path. If you associate sufficient pain to resigning your power in this way, you will come up with more empowering behaviour (just as the rats in Neal Miller's experiment found an alternative way out of the white box).

**Step 2** *Associate pleasure with thinking for yourself.* Imagine yourself thinking your own thoughts, having an idea and carrying it out, and meeting with incredible success. Feel how this energises you. Build this experience up in your mind until it feels real, as if it is actually happening right now. Then imagine the long-term impact it will have on your life.

If you repeat this two-step exercise often enough, you will condition yourself to think for yourself and come to direct your own life as a matter of habit.

## Give yourself permission

Asking for permission is a conditioned habit — break it now. Give yourself permission to live your life in a way that is unique to you. If you dream of running your own business, give yourself permission to do it. If you feel strongly about a social or environmental issue, give yourself permission to speak up, voice your opinion and offer your ideas for solutions. Give yourself permission to experience feelings of pleasure. By practising the suggestions in this book you are making a choice to enjoy life. Give yourself permission to experience feelings you have repressed.

A few years ago I realised I had a lot of anger inside me that I had never expressed because I was afraid to do so. My fear was that if I let out this anger, whoever I expressed it to would also get angry and attack me. I anticipated a counter-blast, as that was what I had learnt to expect in my family. My strategy for years had been to keep silent, to bottle it all up inside and not let on how I felt. On the outside I appeared to be a very quiet person.

I decided to give myself permission to express anger and developed a strategy that helped me feel comfortable with the powerful feeling this gave me. I needed to learn that getting angry was no longer a punishable offence. At the time I was living with a bunch of people who were all into personal growth, so it seemed the perfect opportunity to address this issue in a supportive environment. I let everyone know that I was going to practise being angry around the apartment, which they were quite happy about. Then, one morning, while everyone was quietly having their breakfast, I burst into the room waving my arms around and yelling about the un-washed dishes, the mess on the bench and the state of the floor. They all went into shock. "Just kidding," I said, and got myself some breakfast.

Over the next few weeks I learnt what it felt like to express anger without censure. I learnt that it was safe to let it out, that I — and others — could survive my outpouring. I experienced a lot more energy — the energy I had previously been using to suppress my anger, energy I now channel into creativity among other things.

There is no need to feel guilty for doing what you want. Stop waiting for outside permission. No-one is going to punish you for doing your own thing. Why carry on like the rats in the white box, which continued to behave as if they were going to be electrocuted again but never were? We don't need to fear disapproval that is no longer anything but a memory.

Try the following. State directly what you want — for example, "I want one of those." State directly what you're going to do — "I'm going to go to the beach tomorrow."

Don't say please or give any reason. Avoid the use of questions such as, "Can I have one of those?", "Is it okay if I...?" or, "Do you mind if I...?" Continue like this until you no longer feel any guilt or anxiety. That easy, you ask? Give it a go and see. Remember — do it until you feel no guilt. The fact that you are alive is all the permission you need.

## *Question everything*

Question all authority figures and symbols of authority. Asking questions is probably the most powerful tool you have for taking immediate control of your life and establishing your own authority.

A word of warning, however. Questions can be used to avoid intimacy, to keep people at a distance. I once met a man who continually asked questions, such that it was disconcerting and unrewarding to talk to him for long. Keeping control seemed a life and death issue to him. He was harbouring a lot of unresolved anger towards his parents and ex-wife, which he habitually projected onto others. His biggest fear was being hurt emotionally, so he had erected a strong defence to shield his vulnerability. As we have already seen, if you are motivated to question authority by unresolved resentment and blame, this only serves to trap you in disempowerment. If you ask questions but at the same time don't listen to, or have no interest in, the answers you receive, you are being rude and abusive. Such behaviour will cost you friends and reduce the chances of new people wanting to get to know you. If you are going to use questions as a tool for empowerment, it is essential that you be genuinely interested in what those with whom you are communicating have to say. Asking questions can increase your experience of intimacy or destroy it — empower or disempower you — depending on your approach.

I like to think of asking questions primarily in terms of information gathering. The side effect of being an active information gatherer is that you steadily amass more control over your life and become your own authority. Asking questions sends a powerful message to your brain, which presupposes you are in control. The first person you can ask questions of is yourself. You can start by asking, "What do I want?" You needn't confine this question to consideration of your life goals — ask it in relation to everything, in all situations in which you find yourself. Get clear on what you really want, and make sure that what you are getting is what you want. If you are considering taking out a loan to pay for a car you'd like, be sure that repaying a loan is what you want. You can save yourself time and money — and pain — if, before you become involved in any interaction, you are as clear as you can be on the outcome you are after.

It cannot be denied that there are people who endeavour to force their opinions upon others. This behaviour can be motivated by the need to prove oneself, which in turn can be a result of low self-esteem, self-hatred, self-doubt, guilt, fear of vulnerability or being out of control, or the belief in scarcity, which drives a person to compete. Often our best defence in this type of situation is, first, to know what we want and, second, to ask questions. If someone challenges you, instead of getting angry you can neutralise their challenge with a question and take control of the situation. The skilful use of questions can put you in a position of power and allow you to avoid confrontation at the same time. Question in particular the values that motivate authorities. Many businesses and government departments claim their main purpose is to provide service, while their hidden agenda is economically based. Question rules. Ask, "Is this rule empowering or disempowering?", "Why is it necessary?" and "Who benefits from it?"

 What good fortune for those in power that people do not think

Adolf Hitler

Find out your rights in any situation in which demands are being made of you. You are at liberty to ask questions and expect answers. If you find yourself feeling guilty or anxious in the process, it will be because you are confronting your childhood conditioning. The feelings you had when you stood up to your parents and were punished for it are being stimulated. Press on. The anxiety will pass and you will become comfortable with your new role.

The following is a list of questions you could usefully make a habit of putting:

- Who specifically?
- Who benefits in this situation?
- Who does this apply to?
- Who made this rule?
- Who could offer an alternative?
- Who could be of help?

- What specifically?
- What would happen if...?
- What alternatives can you suggest?
- What is it about... that you don't like?
- What is it about... that you aren't satisfied with?
- What other options are there?
- What will happen if I don't?
- What other possibilities have you considered?
- What are you suggesting?
- What purpose do these rules have?
- What do you mean by...?
- What's stopping you from...?
- In what ways are you willing to...?
- That's a strong opinion. What makes you think that?

- When specifically?
- When does this apply?
- When can I expect to receive...?
- When will you...?

- Where specifically?
- Where did you get that information from?
- Where is this leading?
- Where do we go from here?

- Where can I get the information I need?
- Where did you get that idea from?

- Why specifically?
- Why are you asking me that?
- Why do you need to know that?
- Why is this relevant?
- Why is that necessary?

- How specifically?
- How does this add value?
- How does this affect what I want?
- How can I improve this situation?
- How are you taking my needs into account?
- How can we resolve this so we both win?
- How do you justify...?
- How is that relevant?
- How would you like to be treated in this situation?

- Is that really true?
- Do you have a problem with that?
- Can you be more specific?

## *The question game*

This is a fun way of sharpening your questioning skills. You will need another person to play with. The idea is to see how far you can take a conversation (if that's the right word) only asking each other questions. Neither of you is allowed to answer a question, and if you do, or if you are unable to find a question with which to reply, you start again. Here is an example:

"Would you like to walk down to the shops?"
"Do you think that's a good idea?"
"Is going for a walk a problem for you?"
"What are you going for?"
"Do you need anything?"
"Are you going to get some milk?"
"Do you want some?"

"Will you carry it back?"
"What's stopping you from carrying it?"
"Would you like me to come with you?"
"Where's your pack?"
"Did you use it last?"
"Is it blue with a red band?"
"Where did you see it?"
"Is it over by the dresser?"

By questioning you demonstrate that you matter, that you deserve attention and respect. Playing this game will not only accustom you to asking questions, it will also improve your conversation skills and your ability to reason. As a result you will find you become steadily more confident in directing your own life.

# 9

## *Shaping reality: how you create your experience of life*

WHAT is reality? Very simply put, reality is, for any one person, what that person believes is real and happening. This definition encapsulates two essential points: 1) that reality is an *individual* experience, such that two different people experiencing identical circumstances can nevertheless experience different realities; 2) that this is so because reality is an *interpretation*, an individual's personal *perception* of events, circumstances and the world at large.

Take the two people in identical circumstances. Both possess the same amount of money, say. In this case, one may perceive herself as having an abundance while the other perceives himself as not having enough. Again, the two may be neighbours living in houses of like design and quality. One perceives herself as living in a beautiful environment while the other perceives his environment as unattractive. These two people interpret their circumstances, which are the same, in radically different ways — hence the reality of one is different from the reality of the other. Reality, for each of us, is what we each *believe* is happening to us, for us, around us.

The way in which we each perceive our circumstances, and thus experience reality, itself influences our circumstances — and thus changes our reality. This story from a friend of mine, Sarah, illustrates the point well.

Sarah held a meeting with a number of people interested in attending a training course she was planning to conduct. She left the meeting feeling as if she'd been interrogated by those present, that it had gone badly and that no-one was keen. Motivated by this "reality", Sarah decided to cancel the course, even though that would mean a loss of income and experience. She rang the woman she considered to have been the main antagonist at the meeting to inform her of this decision. On learning of Sarah's intention, the woman was shocked. She had come away from the meeting with a very different view of things. She had found the meeting a great success; she felt she'd had the opportunity to share all her fears about doing the course and was now fully committed to attending. In fact, she had already organised the necessary finances and a babysitter. Hearing this, Sarah decided to run the course after all.

Both Sarah and the other woman adopted behaviour, based on their individual interpretation of events, that had a direct impact on their circumstances. Your current reality — what you have, what you do, your circumstances, and the way you feel about these things — is the way it is because your *beliefs* have caused you to create it that way. What you believe is what you get. This is the essence of the law of cause and effect. Your beliefs are the cause, and the effect is the result they produce in your life. Your beliefs determine what your experience of life will be. The simplest way of expressing this is to say that *your beliefs create your reality*. When you change your beliefs, you change your life. It is that simple. However, the principle of cause and effect isn't something you start using from this point on — you have been using it all along. You don't have a choice about it — you are creative, like it or not. The name of the game is life, the object of the game is to create, and there are no side lines — everyone is in the game. Cause and effect is always operating. At any and every moment, your mind is exercising its creative power. Knowing this, you can become aware of what you are doing.

You will always base your interpretation of the world on your beliefs. The magical thing is, you can believe anything you want. You can choose what you want to see, feel and experience; you are already doing this every second of every day. If you choose to believe you are short of love or money, that life is a struggle, that you have to compete for everything you want or that you aren't safe in the world, you will look around you and interpret everything you see in accordance with these beliefs. On the other hand, if you choose to believe there is an abundance of everything you need and want, that you are loved, that life is exciting and the world safe, you will look around and interpret everything you see accordingly. The world will always present to you what you believe to be true.

Your beliefs can blind you to what is actually taking place. This was illustrated to me when I was taking a walk through the city with a female friend. As we walked, I noticed that quite a few of the attractive men who went past would check my friend out. Knowing she had experienced great difficulty attracting men into her life, I asked her if she ever noticed men showing an interest in her. "No," she said. "Men never show an interest in me." Here was a classic example of the selective power of belief. Men showing an interest in her was simply not part of my friend's reality, regardless of what anyone else might observe. She was interpreting the world according to her beliefs.

Realising that beliefs create your reality, of course, puts you in a position of incredible power. *By changing your beliefs, you can ensure a completely different experience of the world.*

## *The law of extension*

Your mind's function is to extend. Energy naturally travels outwards from its source, influencing whatever it comes in contact with. Energy cannot be contained, it must extend. This is a fundamental principle of the law of cause and effect. Everything you experience is an extension of you. Your creative power extends outwards from you to your creations. This is why it is possible for you to discover your most deeply hidden beliefs by observing the results of what you do. What you have in your life is an extension of what you have in your mind. Your creations belong to you. Your creative energy cannot be contained.

Light, radio and television waves radiate from their source in all directions. Thoughts are no different. We take the law of extension for granted in the natural world. We sit in the sun and "soak up the rays", and we sit around a fire for warmth. We would all freeze if no energy radiated from the sun or a fire. You cannot clap without the sound radiating outwards. If the law of extension ceased to operate, no-one would be able to go surfing as no waves would travel outwards from the storms that create them. In fact, storms wouldn't happen; we'd live in a stagnant universe.

We rarely apply this principle to the human world, to ourselves as energy-emitting entities. Yet humans do emit energy; we set up waves in the energy field in which we exist. These waves travel outwards and influence everything in our environment. Just the act of walking sets up energy waves that, if visible, would look like the wake of a submarine as it moves through water, washing up against objects to the side. Every movement, no matter how small, sets up a vibration in the energy field. Everything we do, including thinking, has an effect beyond ourselves. In other words, the beliefs we entertain in our mind extend or expand beyond us to influence and shape our environment in some way. When we consider our thoughts as creative energy that we are completely powerless to contain, it starts to make good sense to ask ourselves what sort of effect — since an effect of some kind is inevitable — we'd like to have, and what it is we need to think and believe to have that desired effect.

## *Projection*

One way in which we extend our beliefs is by projecting them onto others. Projection is the act of attributing to another person our own personal beliefs, feelings or desires. People commonly transfer, subconsciously, what they believe to be true about themselves onto those with whom they are interacting, thereby judging others as they have already, without realising it, judged themselves. We may have judged ourselves, deep down, as lazy and so judge others as lazy too, regardless of the truth about them. Believing we're bad, we may label others bad. Not recognising our own deep feelings of anger, we may label others angry.

When we criticise others in this way, we are really criticising our own deficiencies. We attempt to rid ourselves of our own faults by finding them in others. Practise being aware of how you judge others and use your judgements to help define any disempowering beliefs you have about yourself. Our everyday speech is a reflection of our beliefs. Becoming more aware of what you say will help you become more aware of what you believe.

 *We don't see things as they are, we see them as we are*

Anais Nin

The other side of the projection coin is that if we honestly believe we are kind and understanding, we will see others as the same, even if they don't see that in themselves. The good we see in others is the good we have in ourselves, although we may not be aware of it. We observe the world through our own beliefs, therefore what we are looking at is a projection of ourselves. Our attitude towards others will always be motivated by our own beliefs. If we want to experience love, we must learn to look upon others lovingly.

## *Generalising*

The projection of beliefs can take on a global scale. We tend to project in a blanket fashion, generalising about the world in accordance with our personal beliefs. Whatever we believe influences our feelings and thoughts about the world as a whole and everything in it. Because the mind tends to work in this way, by making a change to just one belief we can change the way we perceive every aspect of our lives. You might have the belief that you're "not good enough", and apply it to everything, e.g. your house isn't good enough, your family isn't good enough, the movie wasn't good enough. You might generalise the belief "I can't", and apply it to succeeding, achieving, getting what you want, finding a partner, making changes and improving your health. We all generalise with respect to the conclusions we draw about individuals we come across; one experience with a dishonest sales person, for example, and we generalise that all sales people are dishonest and not to be trusted.

If you aren't aware of the beliefs by which you are operating, creating permanent change becomes a never-ending struggle. Many people make the mistake of trying to change the effect without tackling the cause, and this is quite understandable; after all, because we tend to generalise we can easily think it is our house or partner that isn't good enough, or that there is an outside force blocking our progress. But leaving a partner, moving house or blaming others doesn't eliminate the cause of the problem, which is one of personal belief.

Fears, being based on beliefs, also become generalised. People who learn to fear expressing themselves in one way will fear expressing themselves in other, similar ways. Remember how young Albert projected, and generalised, his fear of white rats to similar animals and even objects. When you generalise a disempowering belief, you reinforce it. By defining how you perceive the world, you can create a guide for changing your beliefs. When you find yourself making generalisations, ask yourself, "Is that true or am I generalising my own beliefs?"

## *Beliefs produce feelings*

Feelings are an important part of your personal reality. Every thought you have produces a feeling of some kind in your body. All of your feelings result from your thoughts, which spring from your beliefs. When you entertain a thought, that thought adds a "flavour" to your energy, and the first place your thought-flavoured energy is experienced as it extends outwards is in your body. Different thoughts produce different flavours, and we label the flavours sadness, anger, joy, happiness, etc. These flavours — or feelings — are an immediate and identifiable effect of beliefs.

Beliefs create feelings of disempowerment or empowerment depending on their nature. The beliefs "I'm alone/separate", "I can't get what I want", "I've lost something of value", "There isn't enough for me" and "I miss out" create feelings of sadness. If you believe you have lost, are losing, or are unable to get something you value, you will feel sad.

If you believe you can't get what you want because of an outside influence beyond your control, such as another person, the government or life itself, you will blame that influence and experience feelings of anger. The beliefs "I can't get what I want", "It's your fault", "People don't give me what I want", "Others get what I want", "Life's not fair", "I'm forced to do what I don't want to do", "I have to do what others tell me" and "I have no choice in my life" will all produce feelings of anger on top of your feelings of sadness.

Beliefs such as "I can't do it", "I'm powerless", "I'm weak", "I'm a failure", "I'm not good enough", "I haven't achieved anything", "I can't get what I want", "I don't have what it takes", "I'm powerless to do anything" and "I can't make it" will create feelings of helplessness, hopelessness and powerlessness.

By becoming aware of the feelings you consistently experience, you can define the beliefs that are creating them. *By choosing what you believe, you can feel what you choose.*

You will *feel* powerful and effective when you *believe* you can get what you want and meet all your needs. You will *feel* loved when you *believe* you are loved. You will *feel* successful when you *believe* you are successful. The fact that you are alive can give you feelings of success if you believe being alive *is* success. You will feel prosperous when you appreciate and are grateful for everything you have.

# Beliefs determine behaviour

Just as feelings result from beliefs, so does behaviour. Our behaviour always has its origins in our beliefs, although we may not always be aware of the thought processes involved. Driving a car is an example of an act we often perform without being conscious of the thought processes involved. We can become so familiar with our local roads that we are able to think thoughts unrelated to driving itself. We reach our destination and remember very little about the trip; you could say we've been on automatic pilot. Unless we question ourselves and develop at least a degree of self-awareness, we will live much of life on automatic pilot, drifting along familiar paths, not really aware of the reasons why we're behaving in the ways we are.

Whatever actions you take will always be based on your beliefs. Your beliefs specify the appropriate action in any given situation. If an earthquake struck, I would draw on what I believe such an event means and take the action I deemed necessary. You would interpret the situation in a different way, and hence behave differently. The same earthquake would trigger our actions, but precisely what actions each of us took would be entirely dependent on the nature of our beliefs.

Beliefs, not outside circumstances, determine behaviour. Your actions are always a reliable indicator of your beliefs, even if you aren't consciously aware of what your beliefs are. If I return home to find my house ablaze, what action I take will depend entirely on what I believe it means to lose my house in this way. If I believe it is a tragedy and the ruin of my life, I will behave in one way. If I have never liked the house and have been considering moving anyway, or if I have overinsured it and lit the fire myself, I will behave another way.

Your mind instantly gives meaning to an experience by searching through all the associations you have made that relate in some way to that experience. These associations may stretch far into your past. During this process, your mind will be primarily concerned with deciding whether the experience represents pain or pleasure. If it decides it represents pain, your behaviour will most likely be an attempt to move away from it in accordance with your drive to avoid pain. If, however, your mind decides the experience represents pleasure, your behaviour is likely to be an attempt to intensify or repeat the experience. Your behaviour will be based on what you believe it is necessary to do to avoid pain or to experience pleasure. Even burning your own house down can be an attempt to move away from pain and towards pleasure. You are always free to change the meaning you give a situation, and thus change the way you behave. When you change your beliefs, your behaviour changes automatically to remain congruent.

*Repetition of any word fixes it in mind and causes it to become a moving force in the body*

Catherine Ponder

With this in mind, consider how beliefs can produce disempowering behaviour such as arrogance and aggressiveness. Arrogance can be motivated by the belief that one isn't good enough or is deficient in some way. To compensate for the feelings of inadequacy this produces, a person might claim to be, and act as if, he or she were superior to others in some way. The belief that we aren't good enough can cause us to adopt competitive behaviour. We label others ignorant, slow, thick, incompetent, lazy or ugly in an attempt to raise our own status and hide the deficiencies that, subconsciously, we sense in ourselves. We create an insane competition in which we must win to be okay.

Behaving arrogantly is often a way of protecting ourselves from what we believe is fearful. A fear of change can prompt behaviour that includes closing off to new ideas and claiming our views are the only "right" ones. If we fear intimacy, we can use arrogant behaviour to keep others at what feels like a "safe" distance. We can also behave arrogantly when we are fearful of making mistakes, in which case we act as if we "know it all". Arrogance is the angry cry of a hurt and frightened inner child who is afraid of being hurt again.

Believing others are a threat, or that someone or something may get in our way and stop us from getting what we want, can cause us to behave aggressively. Behaving aggressively is an indication that we do not feel safe in ourselves, that we lack inner security and trust and therefore are unable to feel safe in the world. Arrogant and aggressive behaviour is always driven by the fear inherent in low self-esteem. A person with high self-esteem is not aggressive or arrogant.

Beliefs are the source of all behaviour, and if you want your behaviour to be empowering it must be based on empowering beliefs. If your thoughts are those of self-doubt, self-hatred, fear and anxiety, your body will reflect those thoughts in the way you habitually hold yourself, and you will act and perform tasks without confidence. If you believe you are confident, you will behave in a confident way. You needn't stop there, however. You can act *as if* you are confident right from the start.

How might this help? A large amount of interpersonal communication takes place on a subconscious level. People commonly judge whether or not they like another person even before they have been introduced. Have you ever looked across a room at someone and decided you didn't like them before you knew anything about them? Have you, on the other hand, ever spotted someone and instantly been drawn to them? What was it that made the difference? You might say one was attractive and the other not, but what was it, precisely, that was attractive? Your interpretation of the way they were holding themselves, their facial expressions and their body movements will all have had a powerful influence on your perception. And the way you perceive others — what you believe about them — determines how you behave towards them.

Are you prompting a response from others that you don't really want? Others will always respond to the energy you put out. Have you ever had the experience that people seem to be happier, and to acknowledge you more often, when you are feeling great yourself? When you are up, it shows. You send out a non-verbal message that is interpreted by those with whom you come in contact, who then respond to you according to that message, even though they may not be aware they are doing so.

You are constantly shaping your reality by influencing the responses you prompt from others with your behaviour. You don't need to tell others what you are thinking — your body does it for you. If your body language communicates fear, that will influence the response of others towards you and in some cases might even attract abuse. If your body language communicates confidence, others will respond accordingly, in a positive way. How you hold your body can communicate defensiveness, fear, anger and disappointment, or it can send out messages of openness, safety and confidence. Whether others are helpful or unsupportive is often determined by these messages. You can therefore change the responses you get from others by changing the way you hold yourself. Act confident, even if you don't feel it, and you will prompt behaviour from others such that you *do* feel confident.

To find out what beliefs are motivating your behaviour, ask yourself, "What might I believe that would cause me to act this way?" Then quiz yourself as to what beliefs you have. The majority of your beliefs, even those that are subconscious, can be relatively easily identified by asking yourself searching questions. For instance, in answer to "What do I believe about myself?", list everything that is disempowering; then ask the same question about love, money, relationships, health, other people and life in general and answer in the same way. Your answers will give you the beliefs you will want to change. Now answer the same questions by listing all your empowering beliefs. These will be the beliefs you can reinforce and add to. If you want a smoother life, find out what your beliefs are in advance, before they bring about undesirable events and situations.

Your beliefs about life can also influence the way you breathe. Worrying that "life's hard" and you "can't make it" can cause breathing difficulties or make you take shallow, weak breaths. A belief such as "It isn't safe to let go" can cause you to hold onto your breath. Monitor your breathing during the course of a day; you may be surprised just how often you catch yourself not breathing at all.

By consciously changing how we breathe, we can influence our beliefs about life and aliveness. Because the way we breathe is determined by, and therefore reflects, our deeper beliefs, learning to breathe more fully confronts any disempowering beliefs that are causing us to "hold on" (and thus restrict our breathing). The person who genuinely and devoutly believes that life is an awesome experience to be embraced fully will breathe in a full manner. Full, strong breathing increases the degree of aliveness we experience; it stimulates a passion for life and a sense of being present in our bodies. When we learn to breathe in a full, relaxed manner, free of restraints (as is the case during rebirthing), we start to experience life that way.

Try setting aside a few moments each day to focus on your breathing. If you practise breathing a little more fully on a regular basis, it will become a habit — and noticeably enhance your experience of aliveness.

## We attract according to our beliefs

Energy polarises, like attracts like — in other words, we tend to search out and attract circumstances, situations and people to support our personal beliefs, both empowering and disempowering. We shape our reality by looking for proof and validation of what we believe. This is illustrated by the fact that we tend to seek the company of people with the same, or similar, views, interests or circumstances as our own. Consequently, we can easily think our reality is the only reality there is, because everyone we know seems to share it. Yet huge segments of the population share completely different sets of beliefs and correspondingly different realities. You may think that everyone is changing in the same direction as you and your friends, then you step into another social group and you discover people who are not. What beliefs do you have in common with your close friends?

When you change your beliefs you may find you no longer fit easily into the social group of which you have been a part. When you decide to change, you may want to break away from the patterns that are reinforced by your friends. You can be certain that when you change your beliefs, you will attract new people into your life who will support your new way of thinking.

Often, on the surface, it can seem as if the things that happen to us are beyond our control, but if we dig deeper we find that there is a cause and effect relationship between what happens to us and our beliefs and behaviour. A woman may not at first understand why her partner has left her, but while reflecting on her parents' separation and her consequent loss of a father in early childhood, she may come to realise she is carrying the belief, now subconscious and generalised, that "The men I love leave me." A belief of this kind can have a powerful effect on a relationship. For a start, it can influence the choice of partner in the first place — quite probably a person with a high probability of leaving, being on the rebound from a past relationship or not wanting to make a commitment. The expectation that a partner may leave and the lack of trust this creates can lead to behaviour, subtle and not so subtle, that actually causes the partner to leave.

Things happen to you for a reason, and that reason can be found in your beliefs and consequent behaviour. If you believe that life dishes out "blows" and there is nothing you can do about it, you will indeed experience "blows" and you will have to "cope" as best you can to deal with them. This kind of thinking is only possible if you believe you are a victim of circumstances and that you have no control over what you experience. This is in fact far from the truth. You can treat all unsavoury circumstances that crop up in your life as learning experiences, opportunities to grow and expand, the feedback you need to help you make changes to the way you think and behave.

Everything you do, and every other aspect of your life, is directly related to your beliefs. Your beliefs are demonstrated *comprehensively*. By becoming aware of and defining very specifically the nature of your experience, you can reveal the nature of even your most deeply hidden beliefs.

# 10

## Expectations define your future

*E*XPECTATIONS are specific beliefs about what will happen in any given situation, what will happen as a consequence of specific actions (or a failure to act), or what will happen in the future generally. We have expectations about what it is like to be in a relationship, about how we need to behave while dealing with an authority figure, about appropriate behaviour when communicating with our parents. We have expectations concerning our capabilities and the risks involved in trying new things and making changes. We link expectations of pain to some situations and ways of behaving and expectations of pleasure to others.

Our most deeply held expectations tend to be based on the core beliefs about ourselves and life in general that we formed during childhood as a result of observing and modelling our parents and other significant authority figures. Unfortunately, many of these beliefs are disempowering. We have already discussed the belief "I have to do as I'm told." The expectation that springs from this is that of impending pain if one is disobedient: "If I don't do as I'm told, I'll be punished." Punishment is usually something to be feared; fears are always an expectation of pain. What can be really debilitating — or, conversely, liberating — is that an expectation can influence behaviour such that the expectation is fulfilled and becomes reality.

If we don't take time to assess what we expect of ourselves, of others and of life in general, and address anything we trace which is of a disempowering nature, we will continue to find ourselves in circumstances we would rather avoid. Choosing empowering expectations immediately increases the quality of our lives.

If you expect people to reject you, what do you think the response will be from someone you ask out, considering the disempowering outlook you have adopted is quite likely to show in the way you make your approach by affecting your body language and voice? What degree of self-assurance and confidence do you think you will experience and project? Ask yourself, too, what impact the same expectation is likely to have on your chances of obtaining a loan from your bank manager. If you *expect* to be rejected, will you give it your best effort or are you more likely to say to yourself, "What's the point, I'm going to be rejected anyway"? If you expect the worst possible outcome, don't be surprised if that is what transpires.

 A man can be as big as he wants. No problem of human destiny is beyond human beings

John F. Kennedy

You can change your expectations to change the results you are getting. Business people have long been aware of the power of expectation when setting completion times for a project. If you expect to finish in a week, that's how long it is likely to take. Someone else might expect the same task to take two weeks, in which case that's how long they'll "need". You will perform according to your expectations.

One of my expectations is that I shall always maintain my own car. While I was growing up, my father always carried out his own maintenance. Although he thoroughly enjoyed it, he also had no choice with only a low income and a wife and three young children to support. By modelling my father I took on the same type of behaviour and expectation. Maintaining my own car has been part of my life ever since — and often out of financial necessity while nevertheless giving me

satisfaction.

Another of my expectations for many years was that I had to struggle to get what I wanted. This was so strong that my early attempts at changing it were an immense struggle. A while ago I adopted the counter-expectation that "I'll get what I want but in order to do so I'll have to change." Through experience I have discovered that nothing changes in my life until I change. This new expectation now prompts me to look forward to and even anticipate what the next change will need to be. Another helpful expectation I have developed is that "I'll achieve what I want but to do so I'll have to be committed."

Two children from the same family can develop completely different expectations. A first child may experience his young parents struggling to make it, going without in certain areas in order to save, establishing careers and coping with the all-new experience of starting a family. The second child, born when her family is better established and her parents have bought their own home and achieved a degree of financial security, steps straight into an environment of relative ease and comfort and gets to share in the newly acquired abundance. When the time comes for these two children to go out into the world, the first may expect to struggle over a period of time to make it while the second may expect to make it immediately and without undue effort.

What sort of life are you creating with your expectations? Do you expect to achieve your goals or to be disappointed? Do you expect your relationships to last or to founder? Do you imagine you will find a partner who will love and support you or that you will never find the love and support you want? Do you foresee a long, healthy life or an early death? Do you anticipate a companionable or lonely retirement? Do you expect to have an easy life or to have to struggle for everything you want? What kind of home do you imagine having in the future? How do you expect others to behave towards you? What are your expectations in the area of finance? What about time — to yourself, with your family or partner, for seeing the world?

# *Change your expectations*

Take this opportunity to examine your expectations. Go through the following list and write down everything you anticipate will have happened to you in five years' time:

- My expectations about who and what I will be in five years' time are...
- What I expect to be doing in five years' time is...
- What I expect to have achieved in five years' time is...
- My expectations about my relationships in five years' time are...
- My expectations about my finances in five years' time are...
- My expectations about my health and fitness in five years' time are...
- My expectations about my abilities in five years' time are...

When you have completed this process, read through your list and put a mark next to any expectation that is constraining you in a way in which you don't want to be constrained. Be honest with yourself; if you identify an expectation not to your liking, that's okay, because the whole point of this exercise is to change it.

Once you have been through your list, consider your disempowering expectations one at a time and replace them with new, empowering ones — expectations by which you would like to live your life because they have the potential to produce the results you want. Word these in terms of what you would like to experience. Here are some examples of how to do this:

| *Disempowering beliefs* | *Empowering alternatives* |
| --- | --- |
| I'll be a parent battling with the school system | I'll have found educational support for my children which provides what I want for them |

| | |
|---|---|
| I'll be bored with my husband/wife | Our love will have grown deeper and our life together will be more exciting |
| I'll be sick of my job | My work will be even more exciting and challenging than it is now |
| I'll still be overweight | I'll have learnt how to maintain my desired weight |

Once you have set new expectations for yourself, stay true to them. By settling for less than you would like, you are affirming that you cannot get what you want out of life. Is that something you want to affirm? At times it might appear "so much easier", "only reasonable" or "simply realistic" to settle for less than you'd truly like. It can certainly feel at times as if one is expecting too much. Experiencing doubt on occasion is only natural, however. It can be tempting to give up on your dreams, but if you hold onto your empowering expectations regardless of your doubts, you will eventually get what you want. Don't settle for less.

# 11

## *Changing beliefs: easier than you think*

WE all have the freedom, and free will, to choose empowering beliefs and thereby create whatever we want to create. What are you choosing to believe? It doesn't matter what your current experience of reality is; you have the power to create something different that is more to your liking.

 *Your world is nothing in itself. Your mind must give it meaning*

A Course in Miracles

Every experience you have is created in your mind, even though you may not be consciously aware of the specific belief responsible for a specific experience. If you take the time to practise a little self-analysis and describe an experience as precisely as possible, using your own words and drawing on your feelings, you can determine exactly what the belief is that was the cause of the experience. If you are in any doubt, look to your wider experience of life, which will tell you exactly what beliefs you have chosen.

Changing your beliefs will completely transform your experience of yourself and the world. Having the free will to choose what we want to think and believe, and thereby to dictate our experience of reality, is surely the greatest gift we have. What reality do you want to create for yourself, and what will you have to believe to create it? You can believe absolutely anything. You can think yourself into sickness, pain, loneliness, addiction and complete madness if you are so inclined, and you won't be alone. Or you can think into existence an experience of life about which you feel passionate.

## *Taking the bite out of change*

Among the biggest obstacles you will face when attempting any change in your life are the effects of disempowering beliefs about change itself. Your ability and desire to change are entirely dependent on what you believe it means to change, on your interpretation and expectations of change. What specifically is it that stops you from making the changes you know you'd like to make? You could point to a lack of commitment or consistent effort, but why would you lack these? You could say that deep down you don't really want to change, and that may be true — but why? If you expect change to be painful in some way, this will naturally deter you from making any. If, on the other hand, you anticipated immense pleasure from making the changes you have in mind, surely you would carry them out forthwith.

Some common disempowering beliefs about change are, "It's a struggle", "It's hard work", "It leads to separation", "I can't change", "It takes a long time to change", "Change hurts", "I'll lose my friends if I change" and "It's too late to change." If you have beliefs like these, your drive to avoid pain will guarantee you are motivated to avoid change. But at any time — including right now — you can change your beliefs. If you want to embrace change with enthusiasm, you must associate pleasure with changing and pain with not changing.

First, identify the pleasure that making change will give you. What gains would you experience from adopting new, empowering and supportive ways of behaving? How would you benefit from learning the skills you need to create what you want? Once you are clear on the benefits of changing, you can create yet more motivation by being clear about the cost of not changing. For instance, what is the cost of not stopping smoking? Is the threat of deteriorating health and a premature, painful death enough to be going on with? What is the cost of continuing abusive behaviour towards your children or yourself? What is the cost of not learning the skills required to achieve your goals?

Here is a simple two-part mental exercise that makes use of the drive to avoid pain and the desire to pursue pleasure to help your mind associate pain with not changing and pleasure with changing. Remember — the only reason we resist change is because we have associated it with pain.

First, make a list of all the things you would like to change in your life. Include habits, beliefs, feelings and kinds of behaviour as well as situations and circumstances. Now build in your mind a mental image of the disempowering impact *not* changing these things will have on your life five years from now. Associate pain with not making these changes by taking them one at a time and asking yourself, "What disadvantage, loss, hardship, inconvenience, etc. (i.e. pain), will I experience if I don't make this change?", "What will I have failed to achieve?", and "How will I feel about myself?" Feel how much pain not changing can create. Imagine the detrimental effects on your relationships, health and finances. Imagine how you will feel about yourself and how your self-esteem will be affected. Then imagine the devastating effects in ten years' time, and then twenty. The more pain you associate with not changing, the more you will be motivated to change.

For the second part of the exercise, make a list of the *benefits* you will derive from making each of the changes you have listed. Then close your eyes and visualise making all these changes with incredible ease. Imagine getting *immense pleasure* from making them. Delight in your ability to change. Go on to imagine the empowering long-term effects these changes will bring. Build a mental image of the positive impact making them will have on your life in five years' time. What will you have achieved? How will you have benefited? How will you feel about yourself? How confident and powerful will you feel? Then look ten years into the future, then twenty.

The more pleasure you associate with changing, the more you will be motivated to change.

Once you have convinced your mind that change always leads to greater pleasure, and that not changing leads to greater pain, you will never lack the motivation to change. You will want to change; in fact, you won't be able to stop yourself!

### New, empowering beliefs about change

- Change is easy
- Change is exciting
- Change gives me pleasure
- I love change
- I can change now
- It's always safe to change

# Align your mind with the law of cause and effect

The following is a simple seven-day exercise on which you can embark straightaway to increase your personal power. Set aside a few moments at the start and finish of each day to contemplate the thought presented for that day — three minutes is sufficient — and remind yourself of the thought as often as you can during the day.

### DAY 1: MY POWER IS IN MY MIND

Your creative power lies in your mind. Today's thought re-inforces this concept. Any time you find yourself struggling or forcing a situation, or feeling fear, remind yourself of the power of your mind by repeating "My power is in my mind."

### DAY 2: THE THOUGHTS I FOCUS ON BECOME MY REALITY

Today's thought reinforces the law of cause and effect. Whatever you consistently focus on, you will experience. During

**111**

the day notice what you are focusing on by asking yourself, "What am I thinking about now", and remind yourself that "The thoughts I focus on become my reality."

## DAY 3: I HAVE THE POWER TO DIRECT MY THINKING AS I CHOOSE

The thought for today reinforces the belief that you have free will and can therefore choose your own thoughts. Remind yourself regularly that "I have the power to direct my thinking as I choose."

## DAY 4: MY CURRENT REALITY IS THE RESULT OF PAST AND CONTINUING THOUGHTS. I CAN CHANGE THESE

This thought reminds you that everything you are experiencing is based on your thinking to date and that whatever conclusions you have reached can be changed. Today, every time you notice yourself feeling fear or anxiety, repeat to yourself, "My current reality is the result of past and continuing thoughts. I can change these."

## DAY 5: I'M NOW FREE TO CHOOSE WHAT I WANT TO EXPERIENCE

During your morning practice of this thought, pick any aspect of your life which is not as you wish and ask yourself how you would like it to be. Consider, for example, your relationship with your partner or a friend, your domestic situation, the way things are going at work, the quality or quantity of your free time. Remind yourself of the thought for the day and then ask, "What would I like to experience here instead of what I'm getting?" As you go through the day, stop what you are doing periodically and take a moment to notice what you are experiencing — perhaps a feeling or a situation involving others — and ask yourself, "Is this what I want to be experiencing?" Whenever you answer this question with a "No", remind yourself that "I'm now free to choose what I want to experience."

### DAY 6: MY LIFE CHANGES THE MOMENT MY MIND CHANGES

During today, whenever you notice yourself feeling in any way dissatisfied, or find yourself wishing you had something you don't have or that your life was different from how it currently is, remind yourself that "My life changes the moment my mind changes."

### DAY 7: I CAN CHANGE MY MIND QUICKLY AND EASILY

Today's thought affirms the readiness with which you can change your mind. Each time you remind yourself of this, relax for a few seconds, take a full, easy breath and say, "I can change my mind quickly and easily."

Continue using this exercise until you feel certain about your power to change. You can use it every other week, or start again as soon as you finish the seventh day. Alternatively you can select one of the thoughts and concentrate on it independently. The aim is the same — to implant the seven empowering beliefs in your mind so they can begin to make a positive impact on your life.

## *Reinforcing new beliefs*

We've already seen the reinforcing role repetition plays in the conditioning process. It can help shape a new future — through *re*conditioning — in the same way. Repetition is the key to mastery. Each time you express a new belief or enact a new behaviour, it is strengthened. By continuously reinforcing the beliefs and behaviour you want to adopt, you will ensure they eventually become a part of your life. For example, if you practise asking questions every day, eventually asking questions will come naturally and spontaneously. Repetition is practice; one gets better with practice. Through practice comes skill and ultimate mastery. Repetition, in effect, can take a tiny seed and make it grow into a huge tree. It will move you from where you are now to where you want to be. With continuous reinforcement of empowering new beliefs, your life can only expand.

Don't be fooled by the simplicity of repetition; it is one of the most powerful tools for personal transformation. One of the biggest mistakes people make is not learning the basics. Sometimes someone will tell me affirmations didn't work for them. When I question them I usually find that they only used them for a few days. To produce results you must be consistent and persistent. One of the first affirmations I used was, "My thoughts create my reality." It took a year of repetitive affirming for this principle to sink in to the deepest levels. It finally dawned on me that my thoughts *were* creating my reality, not just some of the time but all of the time. *Any principle you want to live by can be instilled with sufficient repetition, as can any new behaviour.*

I once attended the same seminar on creating relationships eight times, and each time I learnt something different, by making a new and finer distinction. I would take copious notes and immediately afterwards put into practice as much of what I'd learnt as I could. Repetition cemented powerful new beliefs about relationships into my mind, and these new beliefs caused me to adopt new, empowering ways of behaving. Whatever you repeat often enough will become imprinted in your mind.

Your words are constantly doing one of two things: building up or tearing down; healing or destroying

Catherine Ponder

If you start repeating to yourself, "I am powerful", provided you do so consistently, the following things will happen. First, your mind will probably disagree. This is because of the beliefs you already have. Being conscious of this new thought will prompt your mind to seek out any thoughts associated with the idea of being powerful that you already have. If you have beliefs that say you aren't powerful, you will become aware of them. If you continue beyond this stage, the new belief you are affirming will start to make new associations. Your mind will start to link your behaviour to the idea of being powerful and will start to notice situations and events that support the idea of you being powerful. Your mind will search for evidence to support the new belief. Once this is taking place, you are well on the way to change.

Repetition requires focus, and to develop a focused mind also requires — as you'd expect by now — that you practise focusing it. If you focus on being more aware, first you learn to be more aware (because that is what you are focusing on), and second, you learn that the act of focusing improves your ability to focus. Learning requires repetition, which is why it is always best to start doing whatever you want to do *now*. When I started writing this book I was forced to focus on the subject matter, which required that I learn more about it. When you focus on changing, you will learn about changing as you change.

Focusing on, and consistent repetition of, empowering beliefs and behaviour will transform your life. Once a change becomes a conditioned pattern, it will operate without your attention. Do you have to think about how to tie your shoe laces? Of course not — you practised until it became second nature. Learn to enjoy using repetition. Get excited about it. Effective use of all the tools presented in this book can be mastered with repetition.

There are a number of simple but powerful steps you can follow to change your beliefs and, hence, your life.

## *1. Select the belief you want to adopt*

Make your choice by basing it on the result you want to achieve. This can be tangible or intangible. Any belief you have, disempowering or empowering, or any belief you want to adopt, is linked to various associations in your mind. You will tend to become aware of these associations when you start affirming a new belief, which will reveal many of the disempowering beliefs you have been carrying. At first you don't need to think a new belief you want to adopt is true. For instance, you may want to relax into your life more but believe life is a struggle. You may be able to list many reasons why you believe this to be so, and may think statements such as, "Life's easy" and "It's safe to relax" are completely false. This is perfectly normal. The important point is that you *want* the new empowering belief to be true in your life. You will come to believe it is true as you reinforce it and start to live by it.

Nor do you need to fully understand or comprehend the meaning of the new belief you are adopting. How, for example, can you know what it is to commit to something until you have committed? Only through actually doing something do we learn what it really is, so it would be unrealistic to expect to understand the nature of commitment before adopting a belief such as, "I'm fully committed to life." Start simply by choosing a new empowering belief you would like to have operating in your life. To do this, ask yourself, "What results do I want, and what do I need to believe to create them?"

## 2. Build a system of supporting beliefs

To adopt a new belief you need to have other beliefs to support it. One new belief, representing a concept that is foreign to you, stands little chance of being accepted by your mind if it isn't reinforced by other, associated beliefs. For example, if you believe in scarcity you will have an entire network of other beliefs that support that notion. Your mind will have created numerous reasons why scarcity is real. You will have projected and generalised all these beliefs and interpreted everything in your life and world with a scarcity consciousness. One lone empowering belief new on the block stands little chance against an established gang of disempowering beliefs.

To successfully and permanently adopt a new belief you must provide it with back-up in the form of reinforcing beliefs. Once you have selected the particular belief you are going to adopt, draw up a list of supporting beliefs that will add weight to it. For example, the belief "I am confident" could be reinforced by "I feel comfortable in the presence of others", "I feel safe and secure within myself" and "I learn new skills easily." Reinforcing beliefs for, say, "I have plenty" could be "I always have more than enough money", "My needs are always met", "The most valuable things in life are free" and "I see abundance all around me." Ask yourself what other beliefs will help you experience your desired result. In this way you can build a support structure for your selected belief.

## 3. *Reinforce your new belief with reasons*

The key to changing your mind is to give your left brain plenty of reasons to change; the more you can supply, the quicker the change will take place. Whenever you change your mind about something, you do so because it seems a logical choice; whether you are fully aware of them or not, you have reasons that make changing your mind seem like a good idea or common sense. Take the example of witnessing something you didn't think possible; once you have seen it with your own eyes you are forced to believe it. Alternatively you might change your mind when someone whose opinions you respect gives you good reasons why something is so. You can also change your mind when you discover, through your own direct experience, that something isn't as you previously thought; for instance, you may believe a task will be difficult, yet once you have completed it you realise that it was rather easy after all.

Find your own reasons to change. For instance, if you want to adopt the belief "I can create the changes I want quickly and easily", make a written list of all the advantages you can expect by thinking accordingly.

## 4. *Reinforce your new belief with evidence*

The first kind of evidence you can search for is "facts". Search your book shop or library for books containing information that supports what you want to believe. What research has been conducted that bears out your new belief? For instance, it has been proven that there is enough wealth on the planet for everyone to be a millionaire, and the amount of solar radiation that falls on the earth in a day is enough to meet everyone's needs for an entire year. This particular sort of information can be used to reinforce the belief in abundance.

Another kind of evidence is what could be called "creative evidence". Some might consider this wishful thinking, but regardless of what label you apply, evidence of this nature can have a powerful impact on your mind. When on the look-out for creative evidence, remember that anything at all can be interpreted as such. You are free to construe any situation, event, response from others, or object as a demonstration that your new belief system is valid. Given sufficient substantiation, your mind will believe anything you tell it.

When I was building up the assurance in my mind that I was loved and wanted, if anyone so much as glanced at me, I said to myself, "Did you see that? They love and want me." I did this over and over, and within a matter of days I had convinced my mind that it was true, and within two weeks I was in a great relationship. When you think about it, isn't it true that we are constantly searching for evidence to support what we believe? If we think a movie is no good, we look for all its faults to prove our point. In doing so we often ignore the film's attributes. We do the same with people, picking out their strengths or weaknesses depending on what we think of them. A man may see the good qualities in a woman he would like to date, but after being rejected by her starts taking issue with her faults in an attempt to feel better about himself. When you actively search for evidence, you are doing something your mind already does naturally; you are simply speeding up the process by doing it consciously.

### 5. Reinforce your new belief through repetition

Use repetition until you have created certainty in your mind that the belief holds true; in other words, maintain the search for reasons to change and for evidence that corroborates the belief. Bombard your mind with these kinds of reinforcement until the desired change takes place. You will know that your new belief has been firmly implanted in your mind when your behaviour and experience of reality change.

When you change one belief, all your other beliefs are affected; you cannot change anything in isolation. Your mind operates as a system, and change to one part of the system has an impact on all the other parts at the same time. Each change you implement makes it easier to implement others, because they have in effect already been started.

## 6. Feel as if your new belief is already established

How would you feel if your new belief was implanted and fully operational right now? Don't wait. Feel that feeling now. Close your eyes and imagine you have made the change in belief; you are enjoying the rewards, and acknowledging your-self for all the effort you have put in. How does that feel? Now imagine your loved ones responding enthusiastically to the new you, and how that feels. Next, imagine everything you have achieved as a result of this new belief. Feel good? Throughout this visualisation, talk to yourself in the way you would expect someone who held such a belief to do. How does that make you feel?

When we boil it down, we can see that everything we want in life turns out to be a feeling. If you want to be a success, wouldn't you say it's true that you're after a feeling? It's the feelings you get from having money, a great relation-ship, a new car, your ideal home or expressing your creativity that are important.

By this stage, you know what you want to believe (1), you've built up a network of supporting beliefs (2), you've found plenty of reasons to believe it (3), you've actively collected evidence to reinforce it (4), you are continuing the search for more reasons and evidence (5) — and you are now experi-encing the feeling that you expect once the belief is fully adopted (6). If you have done a thorough job of each of these steps, you will already be acting as if your new belief is in place — because it will be.

There is one particular ingredient in this process essential to the guarantee of success — action. Take the steps, rather than just think about them, and you will get results.

# 12

## Perturbation: break through fear and transform your life

*I*MAGINE a city highway system. When it's new, it easily handles the light flow of traffic. Over time the population of the city grows and the number of people using the roads increases. This puts the highway system under stress. Traffic jams and accidents become more and more frequent. Drivers grow frustrated and angry. As the number of cars using the system continues to escalate, the flow is eventually forced almost to a standstill, like rush-hour traffic in a big city. At this point the city either creates a new, more extensive system which can handle the greatly increased volume of traffic, or the increasing chaos and stress cause total breakdown.

Regardless of the type of system, a continual increase in the amount of energy poured into it leads to eventual overload. In this example, energy in the form of cars overloads the highway system. This process is called *perturbation*. Perturbation is the perturbing — i.e. the troubling or shaking up — of a system to the point where it is forced to transform. The same process causes social change. A government is an example of a system that can be transformed through perturbation. When it introduces a controversial law, at first a few people directly affected may protest that the new law is unjust. They write to their local representative but to little effect, as this constitutes insufficient energy to create perturbation (that is, the government remains unperturbed, untroubled). Recognising the need for an intensification of energy to bring about change, these people form an action group, which starts to get publicity. Now the energy starts to mount, and the government becomes aware of discontent and experiences some anxiety. But there is still insufficient energy to create change; more perturbation is required. As the number of people aware of the problem continues to grow, protests are organised around the country and screened on prime-time news. Now energy levels are almost high enough for transformation to take place. Enough people withdraw their support for the government to undermine its power, thereby creating sufficient stress and anxiety to force it to change. The drive to avoid pain is just as valid when applied to governments as to individuals. If a government refuses to change, it isn't re-elected.

Any system that limits further growth, including a belief system, can be transformed into a more expansive system using perturbation. Perturbation is a powerful stimulus to creating personal transformation. You will have noticed that when you make a change, or contemplate doing so, you sometimes feel fear or anxiety; that is, you experience cognitive dissonance. This is a sign that you are starting to perturb your belief system. The reason for this is that you are challenging your beliefs; you are shaking them up. In the case of a limiting belief system, the most powerful way to create perturbation is to apply the energy of action. Action associated with expressing yourself, speaking up and going for what you want will directly confront your limiting fears and cause perturbation. This type of action will put your old belief systems under stress, causing you to experience anxiety. If you keep on stressing the old belief system in this way, it will eventually break down and be replaced by a new system.

Often we may back away from the anxiety associated with perturbation, but for transformation to take place and the mind to reorder we must learn to accept and encourage it as a natural part of the process of change. You can cause perturbation and deliberately create change by doing something that you fear; if you keep doing that thing, your fear will disappear and the change will take place. This is because it isn't the thing itself that is fearful but your thoughts about it. When you act in the face of your fears, you will find they evaporate; in fact, you can move through any fear to an experience of greater freedom. If you put yourself into a situation of which you are afraid, and persevere with seeing it through, you will realise that you are actually perfectly safe and will integrate the experience into your range of capability. A new, more expansive belief system will be formed that associates pleasure with the experience. Your old belief system will be blown away and replaced by one that allows you to function comfortably in the new environment and to explore the new opportunities it brings. Perturbation is an evolutionary process that can create change in your personal life by breaking up old, limiting belief systems, thereby expanding your experience of aliveness and allowing you to move forward with increased power and freedom to express yourself.

## *Little actions produce big results*

Taking little steps on a daily basis can transform your life. Doing something once or twice may not have much effect, but doing something over and over again will redirect your life in the direction you want to follow. Little actions are less confronting, too, and therefore easier to take, yet in the end they yield big results. What long-term difference do you think focusing for ten minutes a day on your goals would make? Probably the difference between achieving them and not achieving them.

Nature provides some excellent examples of the potential of consistent, small-scale action. A tree grows every day, yet if you sit and watch, it appears as if nothing is happening. If you go back to the tree in a week, it may still be hard to tell if there has been any change, but go back in a few months and you will notice a difference. Go back in a year and the growth will be obvious; in five years it will be substantial. The same principle applies to one's life. *If you grow a little each day, eventually you become who you want to be.* Making small but consistent improvements on a regular basis is a powerful way

123

to build and reinforce your faith in yourself. Gradual but steady growth will give you a sense of movement towards your goals.

## Habit busting

One aspect of our lives to which little actions can make a huge difference is our disempowering habits — the little things we do on a daily basis to sabotage our happiness and success. Attempting to change these often creates the anxiety of perturbation, which brings us to the first of three keys to habit busting.

**1.** *Accept the feelings that making change creates.* When you start to change a disempowering habit, in all likelihood you will go through the perturbation process with its associated feelings of discomfort and anxiety. Don't be put off — this is normal.

**2.** *Have a predetermined alternative strategy.* To change any habit you must have a replacement behaviour. Social situations can be tough when you're busting old habits, as these will usually be reinforced by those around you. To become aware of this and to step back from it can be helpful. If you're busting the coffee drinking habit, prepare your response to offers in advance: "I don't drink coffee, but I would like a juice or cup of tea." If you want to stop smoking, use the response, "I'm a non-smoker." If when under stress you automatically reach for food, reach instead for water or go for a walk. Not only is your new alternative better for your health, it is more relaxing. If you have a habit of saying yes to every request, practise responding with, "Let me think about that for a moment", and then think about what you'd really like. Whatever response you decide on, condition yourself to it by repeating it until it feels natural and easy to use.

**3.** *Create the internal motivation necessary to bring about permanent change.* When you are tempted by your old ways, take a few deep breaths before, first, reminding yourself of the pain that will result from continuing the old habit and, second, contemplate the pleasure you will experience from the new behaviour. Once you have associated pain with continuing the old habit and pleasure with the new behaviour, your drive to pursue pleasure and avoid pain will ensure you make the change. Any conditioned behaviour can be extinguished if you cease using it, and to cease using it, it must become an *unattractive* option to you. The more pain you associate with it, the more unattractive it will be. Removing disempowering habits from your repertoire of behaviour will markedly increase your self-esteem.

## *Build momentum with massive action*

When we take massive action, we produce massive change. One of the first fears I decided to challenge was my fear of speaking up. I decided to make overcoming this fear a goal when I volunteered to join about eight other people in promoting a seminar to be led by an international speaker. At our first meeting, each of us had to say our name and explain how we thought our presence added value to the group. While I was sitting waiting for my turn, I began shaking; my fear was so great I almost shook myself out of the chair. Right at that point it hit me loud and clear; something inside said, "Make a goal of overcoming your biggest fear." Then and there I decided I was going to master speaking to groups.

So what did I do? I took every opportunity to speak that came along. Was it scary? You bet. It was full-on perturbation. There were times when I simply couldn't talk; my mouth just wouldn't work. Other times my mouth would dry up and become sticky, and I'd have to use sign language to get a glass of water. When there were no opportunities to speak, I created my own by organising and leading workshops. I kept going because I was determined to master my fear. I *wanted* to feel safe. I *wanted* to be able to relax and be myself with others and in front of a group. And what did I find? Beyond my expectation of pain I discovered immense pleasure. The actions I took created a massive momentum for change which had an impact on other areas of my life I hadn't expected.

What effect do you think overcoming your biggest fear would have on your life? Without doubt all your other fears would be diminished also.

# Start using perturbation now

Follow these simple steps to personal transformation through perturbation:

## 1. Decide what you want

Is there some aspect of your life you feel you'd like to change? Maybe there's a fear you've had for some time, or a habit you've been wanting to break. If you were to describe the change in terms of a goal or outcome, what would it be? For example, if you fear speaking up for yourself, your goal would be learning to do so with confidence. If you fear being alone, your goal would be to master feeling comfortable in that situation. If you are exhausting yourself by being continually on the go, your goal would be to give yourself a break by taking on less or having a rest.

## 2. Decide on an action plan

What can you actually do to achieve the result you want? What behaviour would directly confront the fear that you have? Plan specific steps you can start taking straightaway.

For example, a plan for handling the fear of being alone would need to include setting aside time to spend without company, anything from a few hours a week in a location where you know you won't be disturbed to living on your own. While you are alone you could focus, through writing or purely mentally, on an affirmation such as, "It's safe for me to be alone." You could draw a picture that represents solitude, or contemplate the feelings you are experiencing and write them down and thus learn to accept them.

If your goal is to learn to relax more often, again you must first plan time in which to do so. During your relaxing time, you could identify the fears you are experiencing, or use an affirmation such as, "I'm allowed to relax" or "I deserve time off." Alternatively, you could treat yourself to your favourite pastime — reading, listening to music, taking some exercise, chatting with friends, blobbing out in front of the box with a drink.

## 3. Put your action plan into effect

The energy level of your planned action must be sufficient to overload the belief system you are trying to change. Relaxing for only a few minutes a day won't break the habit of overworking, any more than spending just a few minutes alone will alleviate the fear of solitude. The more energy you apply, or the more intense the experience you give yourself, the quicker the change will come. Use consistent repetition, pouring energy in until your brain makes the shift. You may experience high levels of anxiety, fear and resistance, and be severely tempted to pull back and turn the energy level down. The effort of continuing may seem too much. Limiting beliefs that have previously been repressed may surface, while thoughts such as, "What's the point?", "It's no use" and "I'll never make it" can be a further disincentive to pressing on. If you want to break through and experience greater freedom, however, *you must keep going*. Just before the change takes place there will probably come a point when you feel the maximum frustration and confusion, and resistance will peak. It is at this point that people most commonly give up, just before they break through. Persist now and the energy will soon build to a critical mass, at which stage, all of a sudden, the change will happen. Everything will become easy; your new behaviour will seem natural, as if it's always been that way. You will feel more relaxed and at ease, more expanded and aware. You will have made it.

You may find after you have made a change that the pain that motivated you to make it was far greater than the discomfort of the change itself. The fear of being alone can be most unpleasant; actually being alone can be a real joy.

Often a person will stay in an abusive relationship because the fear of the unknown outweighs the pain of the relationship. Only after taking the leap and finding out that the unknown is not that bad after all, can the person look back and see just how destructive and painful the relationship was. Perturbation is a process — it has a beginning and an end. If you know what to expect, you can anticipate getting through. If temporary discomfort is the price to be paid for power, growth and freedom from fear, it has to be a bargain.

## Overcome the fear of self-expression

In order to express your true self and create the kind of life you really want, you must free yourself from the fear of self-expression. Learning to communicate who and what you are and what you stand for will have more impact on your self-esteem than any other single development. There are several steps to this process.

### 1. Express yourself verbally

Your level of self-esteem will affect the way you use your voice — its tone and volume — as well as your choice of words. Emotions are expressed through the voice, including those produced by a fear of self-expression. Nervousness and embarrassment, for example, can be conveyed by stuttering, hesitation and a tendency to mumble. Changing the way you speak will change the messages you send to your mind. By deliberately injecting a note of confidence, passion and conviction into your voice, you will challenge your old conditioning.

Find a place where you feel safe to practise using your voice. If it makes you feel more at ease, shut the windows and turn up some music. The idea is to get comfortable with using your voice. Start by yelling, "I'm excited!", then shout out all the things you're excited about. Continue for a minute or so, and make it fun. Then give all you've got to, "I feel great! And you know what I feel great about? I'll tell you...", and shout out all the things you feel great about. Then try yelling what you think (in general or about something in particular), what good things you feel you deserve, what you're grateful for, how you're feeling, and how you feel about particular things. If you run out of ideas, tell the wall how you feel about running out of ideas. Say whatever you want in whatever way you want.

As well as using your voice, use your body. Back up what you are saying, and the way you are saying it, by moving your hands and arms. Use body movements to emphasise the point you are making verbally.

Vary the tone and volume of your voice also. It isn't just *what* you say that counts but *how* you say it. Experiment with lifting and lowering your voice at the end of sentences, and by talking both loudly and softly. Experiment with different ways of saying the same thing. How many different emotions can you convey with the same words? The phrase "I love you" can be spoken with passion, gentleness, awe, excitement, even anger and fear.

This is an opportunity to rave on. Go for it. You don't need permission.

## 2. Express yourself physically

The conditioning that creates low self-esteem causes us to control the aliveness we allow ourselves to experience at a physical level. It is impossible to entertain disempowering beliefs without this being reflected physically. We operate as a system in which mind and body are interlinked; hence, by breaking out of stiff, rigid, awkward ways of moving or holding ourselves, we can help free our minds from inflexible and unhelpful ways of thinking.

If you don't express yourself physically with power and passion, it is because of your fears. Fear creates habitually limited patterns of bodily movement. The following exercise will help you move through your fear and break out of those patterns. After completing it you will have a greater sense of physical and mental freedom.

**129**

Choose two pieces of music. The first should be inspiring, something you will enjoy moving your body to by way of warming up. The second should be full-on and outrageous, a piece you can turn up loud. Get into the swing of things by moving around to the first piece of music; then, after you feel loosened up, put on the second piece and dance fast and wild. Move your body in ways you would normally consider out of control. Throw your head around, swing your arms wildly, shake, jump, stamp your feet, open your mouth, hang your tongue out, make silly noises and screw your face up. Act as if you have gone completely crazy. Get lots of energy coursing through your body. Get hot and sweaty. When the music finishes, lie down and breathe; let yourself relax completely, focusing your awareness on the energy pumping through your body.

Repeat this exercise once a week for a few months. Each time you do it, get a little more outrageous. You will be amazed at the benefits you experience.

## 3. Express yourself in a group

An easy way to get comfortable with being seen and heard is to enrol in a class in which you get the opportunity to express yourself. Acting classes, singing and voice lessons, martial arts classes — these are all good examples. Any class will work as long as it gives you the opportunity to practise being expressive in a supportive environment. Taking part will challenge you and create perturbation. It will give you increased power and confidence, and cause you to associate more pleasure with expressing yourself. You will get to have fun. Ring up and book in without delay — it will change your life. If you are already involved in a group, try taking a more active role by speaking up and sharing your ideas more.

## 4. Express yourself to a group

This next step will blast the fear of self-expression out of your life for ever. Get out there and present your ideas to a group of people in a way that expresses all of who you are.

This is one of the most powerful personal growth moves you will ever make. Decide what it is you would like to share — something from your own experience. You could put forward a solution you have found to a life problem, for example — something that will help others add value to their lives. Don't let the thought that you're not good enough stop you; you know that is a conditioned lie. Just the fact that you have the courage to stand up in front of other people will demonstrate to them that they, too, can break out of their old conditioning. You will become competent with practice, so take a trip to the public library and get out a few books on public speaking and making presentations. Set a date and invite your friends along. It doesn't matter if you end up talking to only one person — at least you will have done it. And don't stop there — keep going, and pretty soon you will be able to stand in front of a room full of people and be totally relaxed. Commit to mastering the ability to be totally yourself while in front of people, and your life will expand beyond what you ever thought possible. Challenging your fear in this way will give you an awesome experience of aliveness and supercharge your ability to create the things you want in life.

The process of planning just what you do want, and making it a reality, is addressed in the next, and final, section of the book.

# Part IV

# *Designing your life*

# 13

## *What do you really want?*

WHY is it that often we don't really know what it is we want in life? The reason is related to our drive to avoid pain, which causes us to repress thoughts associated with anxiety. Thinking about what we want, as well as thinking about *doing* what we want, can create anxiety if during our childhood we developed a fear of aliveness and learnt not to trust our own ideas, choices and actions. Once conditioned to do as we are told we associate independent thoughts and actions with pain, and making up our own mind creates anxiety.

If you don't know what you want, the reason is likely to be that you avoid giving it sufficient thought. If you don't give it sufficient thought, a part of you doesn't want to think about it. If you don't want to think about it, you must have associated doing so with pain. If you have associated self-expression with pain, you will avoid thoughts about expressing yourself, including deciding what you want, as deciding what you want is one form of self-expression. This is why so many people avoid giving serious thought to what they want out of life. You cannot know what you want until you think about it. If, on the other hand, you associate pleasure with thinking about what you really want, making decisions and putting them into action, this is what you will do.

If you haven't decided what you really want and have settled instead for something less, you are suppressing your natural drives to explore, express and expand; in other words, you are violating your true self. To do this and still feel relatively okay about yourself, you must find reasons to justify your behaviour. Disempowering conditioning can provide a variety of reasons, a common one being the belief, "I can't get what I want", which has already been discussed. Using this belief it is possible to justify the behaviour of suppressing aliveness by saying, "I can't get what I want anyway so there's no point thinking about it." This is just one example; you are likely to have further disempowering beliefs with which you justify not deciding what you want in life.

Give serious thought to what you want, but don't stop there — actually make a decision and then take action. Once you have decided what you really want, it is the perturbation created by commitment to consistent action that will blast you through your old limits and fears and turn your dreams into reality. When you pursue your heart's desire, you will feel excited and passionate about life — you will have an experience of true aliveness.

## *Disempowering motivators*

The most powerful step anyone can take towards high self-esteem is to turn the dream they have in their heart into reality, yet so many people never do this. To appreciate why, and to prepare oneself to do otherwise, an understanding is required of the various influences that can motivate us to make decisions which result in a disempowering approach to life.

### *Compensatory needs*

Compensatory needs can compel us to do things we don't really want or even need to do. A compensatory need takes the form of a compelling drive to prove we are good, attractive, intelligent, strong, etc., i.e. of worth in some way. We may harbour the conviction that we are unlovable, for example, which creates the need to prove the opposite through compensatory behaviour such as trying to be "the best lover" or having the most lovers of anyone we know. If we feel ugly or unattractive, we may be compelled to attempt

135

to be the most attractive. We may want a PhD because we suspect our intelligence is deficient. Compensatory desires can even motivate us in our choice of career. An unconscious belief that they somehow hurt others can drive some people to become doctors or healers. A belief that they are weak may compel others to take on heavy physical labour or become bodybuilders. A belief that we aren't important may create a desire for positions of authority. A public speaker may act on a wish to be heard that compensates for a belief that no-one ever listens to him. Motivated by the fear that we are wrong, we may develop a desire to be right and aggressively push our point of view. Wanting to own a big car or house, to earn more money, to have the best-looking spouse, to be the most successful, can all be motivated by low self-esteem, as can a preoccupation with looks, clothes, make-up and the latest fashions.

Compensatory needs drive us to attempt to make up for what we perceive as a personal inadequacy. We try, mostly subconsciously, to convince ourselves and others that the disempowering beliefs we have about ourselves are not true. One of the most common beliefs for which we compensate is the *generalised* belief that we aren't good enough. This affects all areas of our lives. Secretly believing we aren't up to something, don't have enough or don't do enough, we attempt to prove the opposite. A businessman who feels he isn't as capable as those around him will continually strive to outperform them at increasing revenue and profits and making his company grow. He is likely to consider his employees unmotivated, because they don't punish themselves in a similar fashion, and is unlikely ever to reach a level of achievement at which he feels satisfied or successful. At home he will be dissatisfied with his wife and feel his children's performance at school isn't up to standard. A businesswoman who falsely believes she isn't good enough may compare herself to men and compete with them aggressively.

Compensatory desires often take on a competitive nature. We measure ourselves against the qualities or skills of others. We compete in an attempt to prove that we have worth and ability, reasoning that if we can beat someone else we will overcome our sense of inadequacy.

There is no question that it is possible to gain a sense of worth by beating someone else, but it is temporary at best. The reason for this is that the belief that prompted the compensatory behaviour hasn't changed, so it doesn't take long for the feelings of inadequacy to return, and for the need to prove oneself all over again to re-emerge.

Compensatory behaviour is evident all around us; if we label someone egotistical, it is often because they are behaving in a compensatory way. If we genuinely believe in our overall worth, however, we have no reason to "prove" it to ourselves or others. Our goals, aspirations and entire life path can be influenced by compensatory needs until we become conscious of the underlying beliefs that are motivating us.

## The quest for love and approval

Many people grow up thinking love is a scarce commodity. It is common to associate the receiving of love with winning or being the best. "Winner takes all" refers to love and attention as well as any material prize. From an early age we learn that the job done best gets the praise, that the right answer gets the teacher's approval and the highest mark. Consequently, as adults we compulsively seek recognition and reward. We work hard and do our best, not out of a passion for life but out of a desire for love and acknowledgement. Yet when we believe we have to be the best to get the love we want, we set ourselves up for endless struggle and disappointment. This is because we are searching in the wrong place for love. Although the Western culture promotes the idea that by being the best we will receive love, this is only on a superficial level as the tragic lives of so many stars, personalities and public figures demonstrate.

We also associate gaining love and acceptance with conforming to others' wishes. Our childhood experiences teach us that in order to get the love we want it is necessary to perform or behave in a certain way, a way that meets with

**137**

approval from others. If we believe love comes from an external source, something that flows from others to us, it follows that if the source isn't happy with us, the love will be withheld or go elsewhere.

> *We grow up thinking of love as a scarce commodity ~ the price in a desperate contest we will enter again and again*
>
> Alfie Kohn

Our choices become influenced by the expectations of our parents and our culture. We go along with others even if in opposition to our own values. Our need to feel we belong can motivate us to join groups with which to identify, to become a greenie, New Ager, corporate executive, sportsperson, Buddhist, Christian, yuppy, academic, football fan, yachty, fashion follower, etc. We adopt the image we believe appropriate. Yet any set of social rules that dictates how one should think, feel, behave and appear can become a disempowering trap *if one is driven by the need to belong*. This can severely restrict the options for creative expression. Rather than choosing one's own unique direction, one is likely to pick a direction that has the blessing of an authority or that will bring the approval of others. If your mind believes that following the rules equals love, don't be surprised if following the rules is what you find yourself doing. Indeed, you will unconsciously search out rules to follow.

## The "have it all" model

The most common perception of success is that promoted by the "have it all" model, which is constantly pushed by the Western culture. According to this model we need to have a huge income, our name in the media, a substantial home in a prominent location, investment real estate, an expensive car and one or more of such extravagances as a yacht, helicopter, racing car, race horse or art collection. How one measures up in relation to this model is graded from having the most (which equals success) to having the least (synonymous with failure). Every product imaginable becomes linked to the model — designer clothes, sunglasses and other accessories; cars, kitchens and electrical appliances; beverages, cigarettes and holiday destinations; lottery tickets, breakfast cereal and toothpaste. The list is endless. Advertisers portray their clients' offerings in such a way as to indicate that by owning or using them we can consider ourselves as moving up the "having" scale of success.

There is only one success ~ to be able to spend your life in your own way

Christopher Morley

The conditioning methods applied to influence our behaviour in this context are the same as those our parents used during our childhood. By repeatedly associating product use with, in the first place, pleasurable *rewards* such as approval, increased status and belonging, and, in the second place, with the alleviation of unpleasant feelings such as inadequacy and loneliness, advertising professionals skilfully manipulate our behaviour by taking advantage of our drives to avoid pain and pursue pleasure. By associating pleasure with having and pain with not having, we are influenced to move in a direction we may not otherwise have chosen.

Advertisers also persuade us by targeting our compensatory needs, by giving us a quick but temporary fix for our low self-esteem in the form of a way to feel good about ourselves. The effectiveness of advertising only serves to highlight the large numbers of people with low self-esteem.

For most of us, our goals, aspirations and expectations have been influenced by powerful outside forces. It's very easy to fall into the trap of wishing for things we don't really want because we think we *should* want them. Are you being unconsciously manipulated by well-planned advertising or are you exercising your own choice? Have you internalised expectations of yourself that can never be fulfilled? Striving to feel successful is a never-ending quest unless you define precisely what success means to you in terms of who you are and what you have already achieved.

The "have it all" model of success is also promoted by some people active in the human potential movement — a movement heavily influenced by the culture of our time. When you next read a self-help book, notice who and what is being represented as a model of success. If the examples are confined to the heads of large corporations, movie stars and sports celebrities, then no matter what else the book has to say, it is promoting the same disempowering model. And don't stop there — go on to check what aspect of the models' lives is being discussed. Are you being told how happy they are, how high their self-esteem is, how harmonious their relationships are, or how healthy and fit they are? Or are you being told how they made it financially, how much money they have and how quickly they managed to get it? All too often the hidden message is, if you don't have the money you're not good enough and so here are the techniques to help you get it. Having a lot of money and possessions won't cause you to experience self-worth or happiness. Having huge amounts of money — or being better than others — isn't a determiner of high self-esteem; in fact, it is often a form of compensatory behaviour for low self-esteem. It isn't that it's *bad* to have a lot of money and possessions; the point is that we need to be clear as to our reasons for choosing and pursuing our goals, material wealth included.

The "have it all" model of success is extremely seductive; it is built into the very fabric of our society and is rarely questioned. It is practically impossible to avoid its influence. It encourages conformity, as everyone learns to value the same things; it also encourages competition, which keeps consumer sales moving. If you have the latest gismo and I don't, in order for me to be as good as you, I need one too. If I get the next model, you fall behind. "Having it all" implies being the best. We may laugh at the idea of "keeping up with the Jones's" but how many of us are unwittingly attempting to do just that? "You can have it all" encourages dissatisfaction with what we already have, because it presupposes we are deficient. The logical conclusion is that this model will never satisfy. It cannot deliver ultimate satisfaction because its message is that we haven't got enough — however much we *do* have. To experience fulfilment, it is necessary to believe one has everything one needs and wants.

It is up to you to decide to what extent, if any, you use the "have it all" model to measure your self-esteem and success. I wouldn't deny that it is a real challenge to disassociate one's sense of self-esteem and success from how much money one has, what one looks like, what car one drives, etc. My purpose here is merely to point out some of the shortfalls of using this particular measuring stick. *As long as your self-esteem and sense of success are dependent on external criteria, they are at risk.*

Ask yourself, "What is my own unique definition of success?" The challenge is to redefine success in your own terms. Make the time to do this quick exercise. Write "My requirements for success" at the top of a blank page, then list everything you currently believe it is necessary for you to have, be and do to feel a success. Don't try to be "enlightened" at this stage or censor your thoughts — write down what your mind comes up with spontaneously, both empowering and disempowering. Fill the page. When you have finished, review what you have written and now take the time to think. For each point ask yourself, "Is this *really* important to me?" If it isn't, put a line through it. If you think it *is* important, ask yourself, "*Why* is this item important to me?" Then ask, "Are these *my* reasons, or are they *conditioned*?" As a final step, see if you can come up with some alternatives that are a more faithful expression of the *real* you.

## The family model

The family also offers a model of success, although in many cases it might be more accurate to call it a model of survival. As children we often express a desire to grow up to be just like Mum or Dad. Because what our parents do for a career or with their lives is so familiar to us, it is easy to follow the same or a similar path, especially if we are actively encouraged

to do so. Encouragement acts as positive reinforcement —
we get more love and approval if we please our parents or if
our actions don't threaten them. We may be quite happy
following our family model, starting our own family at the
same age as our parents, forming a relationship with a partner
similar to our parents', continuing with the same attitudes
and opinions. On the other hand, we may not.

It may be that we follow our family model because to do
so is to "go with the flow". When we unconsciously go with
the flow we are choosing to conform, and choosing to conform may be choosing the disempowering aspects of our family model. This is a clear demonstration of a lack of self-trust.
The story, told by a friend of mine, illustrates how going with
the flow can influence our choices:

> All of a sudden I found myself at high school. I remember not
> wanting to grow up. I can't remember who made the de-
> cision but I ended up in the shorthand–typing class. I didn't
> know there was a choice and wondered why other students
> were doing French and Latin. Anyway, I did really well at
> shorthand–typing; in fact, I was first in the class four years in
> a row. I remember getting lots of approval from my parents
> for my good marks. I was under the impression that I was
> going to high school so I could get a job. The shorthand–
> typing teachers were constantly referring to the time when
> we would become secretaries. I didn't realise at the time that
> I could go on to higher education. I didn't know doing well
> also meant I could go to university. My teachers and my
> parents both encouraged me to be a secretary and I went
> along with that. I left school and got the first secretarial job I
> applied for. I hated it; I was continually correcting the
> accounting figures submitted by the branch managers and
> getting no credit for it. I didn't like being my boss's tea lady.
> I stayed six months, during which time I discovered there
> were other jobs that people do. I thought I'd like to be a
> nurse, teacher or social worker, but my parents and
> grandparents told me that because I'd learnt shorthand–
> typing I had to give it a decent go. So I did. I was very good

*at what I did, so one job led to another and I quickly moved up the ladder of secretary-land. Even though it was never what I really wanted to be doing, I didn't stop until fifteen years later, when pain finally forced me to. I developed occupational overuse syndrome. I'm sure the build-up of resentment and anger contributed to my injury. During those fifteen years I constantly felt out of place, clotheswise, attitudewise, intelligencewise. Once I had stopped working as a secretary I went to vocational planning to help me change direction. After numerous psychological tests they told me I'd been a square peg in a round hole all those years. Now the struggle is over; I'm no longer willing to conform! I now have a degree in psychology and am getting on with what I really want to do.*

It can be very easy to let the general flow of things carry us along, and the further we go down the path the harder it seems to step off. The lesson here is that one must choose one's own direction, and the sooner the better. If you don't set your own course, you can be sure others will set one for you. How long will it be then before you finally start doing what you really want to do? Will you hang out until pain forces you to change? How would it feel looking back at your life knowing you hadn't had the courage to do the things you really wanted to do? Check your aspirations. What are your dreams, and is what you are doing bringing their realisation any closer? *Make the change now.* Don't put it off any longer. You have nothing to lose and *everything* to gain.

## Perceived lack of choice

Have you ever made a choice because there seemed to be no alternative? Most of us have. When I was at college, I wanted to be an architect but didn't believe I was smart enough. My only choices seemed to be drafting and art. Although I enjoyed, and was good at, art it wasn't considered a serious career option. That left drafting, which didn't exactly light my fire. This undoubtedly led to my eventual poor marks in

**143**

the subject. I left college in a dilemma as to what to do. I enjoyed playing with cars and some of my friends worked in the automobile industry, so I applied for two apprenticeships, one as an auto mechanic and the other as a car painter. I was accepted for the painting apprenticeship, which pleased me. I figured it was more creative than lying under a car getting covered in grease.

The point is that I believed I had very little choice. I wasn't aware of the almost endless career opportunities in the greater area of art. It didn't occur to me that it was someone's job to design packaging, illustrate books or create advertising images, or that there was such a position as art director. Often we are ignorant of the opportunities that are all around us.

There is no lack of choice, but there is lack of awareness of choice. Even if we recognise that choices exist, however, low self-esteem can stop us from pursuing them. Don't let the belief in lack of choice limit you. Ask questions, do some research, find out what the possibilities are. There are always possibilities that we haven't yet thought of.

Occupation is just one area in which people's decisions are often influenced by a perceived lack of choice. Money is another. Basing decisions solely on a "need" for money is almost certain to guarantee unhappiness. "I had to accept the job, I needed the money." Heard that before? It's a close relative of "I had no choice." A more empowering approach is to figure out what you really want to do, then employ your natural creativity to find a way of making money doing it. Ask yourself, "Who is producing an income from doing something similar to what I want to do?" or, "In what ways can I generate an income doing what I really want to do?" Your mind will answer any question you ask it. If you use your creativity, you can do what you'd love to do *and* have money.

## Self-doubt

Doubts about your ability will influence the decisions you make. What sort of effect do you think beliefs such as, "I'm not good enough", "I'm not intelligent enough", "I'm stupid" and "I can't make it" are likely to have on your choice of goals? Wouldn't you agree that such beliefs would motivate you to hold back, to attempt only those tasks you already know you can achieve? What you believe is beyond you, you won't attempt. Most people underestimate what they are capable of. Should you do likewise, it will obviously limit you in creating the kind of life you truly desire. Consider the long-term cost you will pay in terms of the quality of your life if you continually doubt your ability.

Imagine, on the other hand, the impact on your life of a firm belief in your ability to master anything to which you set your mind. Are you confident at present that you could learn new skills? Do you feel able to make your mark in an empowering way? When we believe in our own ability to learn and grow, a world of opportunities opens up. The possibilities are countless. If you had total belief in your abilities, what impact would that have on your decisions? Would you take more risks? Would you go for what you want? Would you jump at the chance to acquire new skills? Your personal beliefs about what you are capable of have a direct impact on the choices you make in every area of your life.

## *What I really want is... but...!*

When we go against our true selves — that is, when we make decisions at odds with, and act in a manner contrary to, our real, albeit hidden, inclinations and desires — we know we are doing so, even if only deep down. We experience discomfort. Rather than challenging ourselves and striking out for what we really want, all too often we make justifications for conforming, for taking the easy way out, for not changing. We have already discussed how the discomfort we call cognitive dissonance can cause us to adopt a new belief. If fear stops us from doing what we want, we will find reasons to justify our behaviour. If, for instance, we work in an office and hate every moment of it yet are too scared to make the change to doing what we'd really like, we justify staying in the office with beliefs such as, "I need the money", "I'd have to take a drop in pay and I can't afford that", "I have to pay my mortgage", "It's all I know how to do and it would take me too long to learn new skills", "It's hard to get a good job; you have to take what you can get in today's economic climate" and "I'd rather live in the country but it's harder to get work there." Working at a hated job is a classic demonstration of low self-esteem. Use justifications often enough and you'll end up believing them; they'll trap you and cause you to make disempowering choices. Such beliefs express fears and diminish one's creative power. Justifications will strengthen any fears that are stopping you from pursuing your dreams and desires; they will add weight to them. Justifications reinforce low self-esteem.

The problem of low self-esteem starts with the denial and abuse of one's true self and cannot be resolved by more of the same. The fastest way to create high self-esteem is to follow your true self — that is, to listen to your intuitive thinking and act on it. Take action *now* and carve out a life of your own; there will never be a better time. When you take action, you will quickly move beyond old limits. Your fears will diminish and your sense of safety and freedom will expand. There will be only success and growth; you cannot fail. Start expressing your true self by choosing the direction in which *you* really want to go — with no ifs or buts.

Your future stands before you — what's it going to be? The choice is yours.

It is an act of worship just to sit and look
at high mountains

Sir Edmund Hillary

# The key values of high self-esteem

The values you choose will determine the level of self-esteem you will ultimately experience. By adopting the specific values that are essential to high self-esteem, you can immediately raise your own self-esteem and thus the quality of your life.

## Self-knowledge

Self-knowledge, which can be taken to embrace personal growth, self-education, learning from every experience and the drive to understand oneself, is an essential ingredient of high self-esteem. It forms the basis of an appreciation of who and what one is at the deepest level and eventually leads to self-mastery. Through the quest for self-knowledge you will discover how you have become who you are, and your power to change. If the path of self-knowledge is consistently travelled and the discoveries made along it are acted upon, rapid improvement in one's life circumstances follows. To experience changes that are of one's own doing is a powerful builder of self-esteem.

Link your desire to achieve to the value of self-knowledge. The more you understand yourself the more you can use that understanding to change and grow, and the more power and resources you will have to fashion your life the way you want it. In order to improve the quality of your life you must constantly grow and expand — in other words, increase your self-knowledge. Greater self-knowledge will allow you to make better decisions based on your true desires and aspirations.

## Love and self-respect

High self-esteem rests on a solid foundation of love and respect for oneself. You must be committed to giving up self-denial

**149**

and self-violation if you are to experience high self-esteem. Every day you must learn to treat yourself with ever-expanding love and respect.

## *Freedom*

Freedom is a vital element of high self-esteem — freedom to express oneself, to explore life and to grow and expand. Valuing the freedom to express your creativity and ideas, and the freedom to think for yourself and choose your own actions — i.e. the freedom to be who you want to be — is basic to high self-esteem.

## *Aliveness*

We all want an experience of aliveness, to feel vital and healthy, to feel excitement and passion in our relationships, our work, our environment and our lives generally. You wouldn't be reading this book if you didn't want to increase your level of aliveness.

> ...the human being is so constructed that he presses toward fuller and fuller being and this means pressing toward what most people would call good values, toward serenity, kindness, courage, honesty, love, unselfishness and goodness
>
> Abraham Maslow

## *Courage*

Courage will move you to question your thinking and behaviour, to break disempowering habits and step into the unknown. It takes courage to constantly stretch yourself. Without the courage to act, nothing changes. It is courage that will build your self-esteem and move you beyond your fears.

## Flexibility

Flexibility is essential if you wish to make personal changes quickly and easily. Growth depends on changing your mind, changing your perception, changing your behaviour, all of which are impossible without flexibility. You need to be able to let go of old ways of thinking and behaving and embrace the new.

It isn't only on a personal level, where the beliefs and values we have modelled from our parents may no longer be appropriate in terms of our ability to create what we want, but also in a social and cultural context that we need to question our values. The massive cultural changes that Alvin Toffler spoke of in *The Third Wave* are in full swing.* In our lifetime we will witness radical changes in values. Many of our current cultural values will cease to be valid. The way we do things is always changing and expanding, and our conception of how matters stand needs constant updating.

Flexibility is a key value for navigating these times smoothly. There are more and more models of what it is possible to do, of how to live and work, what it means to be a family and how to manage a country. People are expressing their individualism and uniqueness in growing numbers, and this creates even greater opportunities for self-expression, opportunities to custom-design our own lives; yet we can only take advantage of these opportunities if we value and cultivate flexibility. Without flexibility and open-mindedness we will feel threatened and withdraw into ourselves, building defences to keep out what seems to be an increasingly hostile world.

# Define your values

As well as the values essential to high-self esteem, which together make up one of the foundation stones of a truly fulfilling life, there are those that pertain to other aspects of our

---

*The Third Wave: The revolution that will change our lives, Collins, London, 1980

existence and are a matter of individual preference. Values are the criteria upon which we base our decisions. Should you value privacy, this will influence your choice of living arrangement; should you value honesty, this will influence the manner in which you approach relationships. What are the values by which you would like to live? Check these and you will start to define the direction in which you would like to go.

Work through the following sections, specifying your values and putting them into writing. Writing, rather than just doing the exercise in your head, will force you to think clearly and express yourself precisely.

The questions provided are only examples to get you started; there are many more you can ask yourself.

## 1. Relationship values

What is important to you in your relationships? Do you value honest communication? What about support and encouragement? Do you consider it important that the people who tend to be around you most often share your enthusiasm and passion for life? Is a shared commitment to growth high on your priority list?

## 2. Career values

Is it important that you be able to set your own timetable? Must your work give you opportunities to promote your personal growth? What sort of work environment do you value? Is working outside an important consideration, or do you prefer a comfortable office? Is working from home something you value? Do you like working alone or with others in a team? Do you enjoy physical work, mental work or a mixture of both? What sort of financial rewards do you expect?

## 3. Home values

What value or qualities would you like to be represented in your home? Is it important that home is a place of peace from the outside world? Do you value privacy? What about self-sufficiency (e.g. growing your own food or harnessing solar energy)? Do you want a home designed to handle social activity so you can entertain easily? Is low maintenance a must? Do you value light, sunshine and warmth? How much, and what kind of, space would you like? What about setting and aspect? Or a country versus a city environment?

## 4. Health and fitness values

What are the considerations that play an important part in helping you attain and maintain the level of health and fitness you desire? What sort, and quantity, of daily exercise do you value? How much sleep do you consider essential? Is diet of particular importance to you? Would you prefer to eat only organically grown food? Do you enjoy keeping up with the latest advances in health research? Maybe you value having regular holidays for relaxation and inspiration.

## 5. Financial values

What is important to you when it comes to your financial life? Clearly defined values can take a lot of stress out of financial dealings. Good communication, honesty, prompt payment of accounts, using cash instead of credit, budgeting, saving — these are just some of the options you can usefully consider.

## 6. Leisure values

When you're taking time out, what sort of experiences do you value? Do you like to relax at home or to head for the wilds far from town? Maybe you value privacy, spending time during which you know you won't be disturbed, or prefer doing something in the company of others. How active or passive do you like to be? How physical or mental?

# 15

## *Ideals are achievable*

*T*HOSE who say ideals aren't achievable are the least likely to have had the courage to try. There is no better way of creating high self-esteem than creating a life that you love. If you enjoy everything you have, do and are, you cannot help but feel great about yourself. Your self-esteem will grow through going for what you really want. Once you have defined the values by which you wish to live, the next step in creating the life you want is to define your ideals. Taken together, these represent what you consider to be the perfect experience of life. You could think of them as your ultimate destination, or the big picture of what you want. They embrace all the qualities you value most highly. Your ideals should excite you and give you the motivation to take the action that will make them a reality.

Defining my ideals has had a profound impact on my own life. As I have already mentioned, some years ago I was feeling very alone in the world. I didn't believe anyone wanted to have a relationship with me or to love me. I was too afraid to ask anyone out on a date because I was sure they would reject me and I wanted to avoid that pain. I also believed I was unattractive. If you think this sounds like a lousy experience, you're right. But the time came when I decided things had to change, and I knew that if that was to happen I had to be clear on what I wanted, so I asked myself, "What would my perfect experience of relationships be like?" I decided I wanted to feel confident communicating with others. I also wanted to feel that people liked me and were interested in getting to know me. I wanted to feel attractive, and as if I had something to give. Then I asked myself what beliefs I needed to adopt to make my ideal experience a reality. Among others, I seized upon "I am loved and wanted as an attractive man" and "People are eager to know me." I used consistent repetition to reinforce my new beliefs, as well as looking for evidence that they were valid, and pretty soon things started to look up.

Once I was experiencing an encouraging degree of success and confidence in my relationships, it was time to get more specific and decide what I wanted in my ideal intimate relationship. I asked myself, "What do I want in the woman I'm going to share my life with?" After carefully considering my values, I decided I wanted a woman who wanted me unconditionally and who I wanted unconditionally. She had to be someone who excited me physically, emotionally, mentally and spiritually. She had to share my level of commitment to personal honesty, self-awareness and growth. She also had to value simplicity and nature. I wanted a relationship with lots of laughter, outrageousness and passion. Above all I wanted being together to be easy and fun. Once the full picture was clear in my mind, I locked onto it. I kept my vision alive by constantly imagining what it would be like sharing my life with this woman. I imagined she was beside me when I was in my car. I held imaginary conversations with her. I couldn't help but get excited about her. And now — need I say? — my ideal is reality.

What would it take for you to get excited about your life? What would your ideal experience of relationships, career, your home, leisure and finances be? What sort of life would you create if you thought of yourself as an artist setting about a masterpiece? Would you chisel it out of stone? Would you use oils, pastels or watercolours? Would you use fabrics or some other material? Would it be smooth or textured? Would it be a masterpiece of words and music? You can continue to do things in the same old way, or you can choose new, exciting alternatives that express your uniqueness and potential.

It may not happen overnight — but it will happen. Your life is the greatest work of art you will ever have the opportunity to create.

# Define your ideals

Define an ideal and you are halfway to realising it. By following through with consistent focus on its attainment, you will undoubtedly get the rest of the way. Ideals *are* achievable — so be an idealist.

> The vision that you glorify in your mind, the ideal that you enthrone in your heart — this you will build your life by, this you will become

James Allen

In the same way that you have already defined your values, write down the specifics of your ideals. Use your values as the criteria upon which you base your choices; that is, as you define your ideal experience of each area of your life, ask yourself, "Does this take my values into consideration?" or, "If I was to have this experience, would my values be violated?" By asking these questions you can ensure your ideals are a true expression of the values according to which you would like to lead your life.

## 1. Ideal intimate relationship

Relationships can be fun, passionate, nourishing, supportive, inspiring, fulfilling, loving and easy. A relationship can offer a secure environment in which to open up to greater intimacy, love and honesty, and to establish a much deeper understanding of oneself and each other.

You may wish to define a relationship with someone you have yet to meet, or to define how you'd like your relationship with your partner or another close friend to be. If you are defining your ideal relationship with your partner, you will both benefit greatly from doing this exercise together. Not only will you get to know each other better, you can use it as an opportunity to introduce some of the elements you'd like your relationship to have, e.g. more honesty, fun or excitement. How do you want it to feel? What values do you have in common? What do you both enjoy doing? How would you describe the partner of your dreams and your relationship with him or her?

## 2. Ideal career

In the Western culture we have created a mind set that says work, as a rule, is something we do for forty hours a week. We have developed a belief system about what each hour is worth and the number of days a year to be set aside for holidays. We have formed a model of what we tend to assume is the only option, but this model is only a creation of our minds. We can change it if we want to.

We can, if we wish, create a ten-hour working week that gives us ample income if we use our creativity. We have created the current system, we can create something else. What if you based your career on following your curiosity? That's a big difference from basing it on what you think you have to do to survive. Which do you think would be more exciting — following your curiosity or working for survival? When we work to survive, it's a chore. If your work doesn't excite you, you're wasting your time and your life. Curiosity leads to contribution, and contribution creates wealth. Committing to following your curiosity will take you in the direction your true self wants to follow. What would happen if you continually asked, "How can I create a job I love?" Your mind will find an answer to any question you ask it. How about , "What am I curious about right now, and how could I make that part of my career?" You can create an occupation that is fun, easy and financially rewarding; there are virtually no limits except those you impose upon yourself. Work can challenge, excite, inspire and stimulate growth.

What rewards — other than financial — do you want from your work? Work is an opportunity to express your uniqueness, make a contribution to humanity and put your individual stamp on the world. What would make you feel fulfilled? What would be the ultimate for you? What value would you like to add to the lives of others? How much time would you devote to it? Do you want to be self-employed? Do you have particular skills you'd like to improve? Do you want lots of responsibility? What have you always dreamt of doing? If there were no restrictions, what would you be doing?

## 3. Ideal home

Having a supportive, safe home environment is imperative to mental wellbeing. It offers more than shelter; it can be a sanctuary where we relax, feel comfortable and nourished and escape the craziness of the world. Home is somewhere to which we are eager to return.

What features would you like your home to have? Would you feel inspired if you could see mountains from the front room? Does being close to the ocean or a lake turn you on? Is living in an environment where you can enjoy clear air and wake up in the morning to a chorus of birdsong important to you, or do you prefer the buzz of a big city, with cafes and entertainment near by? What area do you have in mind? What would be your ideal location? What kind of building would you like? There are so many options, from a tent to a high-rise apartment, from mud brick to high-tech plastics. What about decor? What colours do you like? What facilities do you want? Do you hanker for big windows that let in lots of sunshine? Do you enjoy gardening? Would you like a spacious, well-equipped workshop? What would your dream home be like and what would it contain?

## 4. Ideal health and fitness

Our state of health and fitness has an impact on our ability to function mentally as well as physically, and on how we feel about ourselves — that is, on our self-esteem. There are many people of unsound health who live fulfilling lives, but there are probably many more who do not. Certainly those who enjoy a high degree of health and fitness — or could do so with a little effort — are blessed with an advantage, an asset it would be foolish to waste.

> Walking isn't a lost art ~ one must, by some means, get to the garage
>
> Evan Esar

Daily exercise is essential for good health. As you undertake to achieve your chosen level of fitness, it is important that you build up your stamina gradually over a period of time. If you haven't been exercising recently, your body will need time to adjust. Regular exercise, a little each day, is the safest and fastest way to fitness.

What level of fitness do you consider your ideal? What activities or training do you want to commit to? How would you describe your ideal state of health? What would be your ideal experience of your body? How do you want to feel about it? What foods do you want to make a part of, or eliminate from, your daily diet?

## 5. Ideal financial situation

What can you do to help yourself relax over money? A person's real worth isn't measurable in financial terms, but everyone deserves to have enough to meet their needs. Money will conform to the beliefs you have about it; any experience you want to have of money, you can have. A woman in one of my workshops told how she grew up believing money grew on trees, a belief to which she attributed in part the ease with which she had attracted money in her adult life.

How do you want to feel about money? Do you want to be financially independent and self-supporting? How much money do you want to earn? Do you want a smooth-running budget? How much do you want to save each week? What investments would you like?

## 6. *Ideal leisure life*

Leisure is often considered something we get round to only when we have the time. This needn't be the case at all; indeed, leisure is a vital part of a healthy lifestyle. In Western society it can be essential to one's sanity to cultivate laziness. It is all too easy to get caught up in the day-to-day rush and urgency of making a living. It can take a high degree of self-esteem to do nothing if one isn't used to it. Why not master the art?

Leisure gives us an opportunity to recharge our batteries and contemplate our lives. Without leisure, creativity is likely to dry up. When I go out to an isolated beach for a surf, I often come home filled with inspiration and new ideas. Sitting out in the water, immersed in the awesome power of nature, can be a humbling and spiritual experience — one that reminds me what is really important to me.

What would be your ideal experience of leisure? Brainstorm all the activities you enjoy or would like to make a part of your life. Include the simple things that give you pleasure and all those you haven't done but would like to. You might want to give yourself a mix of energetic and restful activities, e.g. tramping, windsurfing, golf or skiing, and reading in the bath, watching *The Simpsons* on TV, listening to music or enjoying a glass of wine by candlelight. Perhaps you have a hobby of some kind — tinkering with your car, photography, cooking, making home-brew or playing a musical instrument. The possibilities are endless.

It is important that you give yourself permission to enjoy yourself and actively plan for pleasure. If you aren't setting aside time specifically for pleasure, what does that say about your beliefs? Being conditioned to do authority's bidding is probably causing you to avoid pleasure by making you feel guilty whenever you experience it or think about it. On the other hand, if you believe you deserve pleasure, you will plan for it.

Not only must you plan for pleasure, you must budget for it too. If some of the things you want to do cost money, make a habit of putting enough aside on a regular basis so it is always available. There is nothing as disempowering as deciding you want to do something then telling yourself you don't have enough money. Create the financial resources you need.

Give yourself pleasure now by defining your ideal leisure life.

## *Create a vision*

Now you have defined your ideals, put your imagination to work. Picture yourself living your ideals as if they are already true. Your imagination is one of your most valuable assets; you can use it to create a vision that will draw you forward. Motivation is dependent on imagination; we all need something attractive to work towards. Imagination inspires action. One of my dreams was to share my ideas by writing a book, even though I was unsure how to go about it. By consistently focusing on my vision, I built the foundation that eventually led to its realisation.

Focus on your ideals daily to create a powerful, compelling vision of your future that will draw you bit by bit towards its materialisation. By constantly reinforcing your ideals you will send a powerful message to your brain about what you want. Make your ideals real in your mind by bringing them to life with colour, action, sound and feelings. What would it feel like to be living your ideals now? What would you be doing? Where would you be? What sounds would you be able to hear? As your vision grows in strength, so will the power it exerts over your behaviour. You will find yourself spontaneously making decisions and taking actions that support the manifestation of your ideals.

 Live by intuition and inspiration and let your whole life be a revelation

Eileen Caddy

**161**

# *Align your beliefs with your ideals*

With your ideals defined and your imagination working on the vision of the future they provide, the next step is to remove any limiting or disempowering beliefs that could sabotage their realisation and replace these with new beliefs that will support the forward process. Ultimately, it is our beliefs that determine whether or not we make our ideals a reality. It is the beliefs we entertain on a consistent basis that are responsible for our everyday experience. Beliefs can destroy dreams or make them come true. Doubts about our ability, belief in the inevitability of struggle, and fear of change all have a detrimental influence. Take your ideal career, for instance. This is probably quite different from anything you have done before, and some of your old beliefs may not be supportive of creating this new experience. By identifying those limiting beliefs and exchanging them for empowering alternatives, you can guarantee the realisation of your dream career. Follow these steps, in writing:

## *1. State your ideal as a goal*

This is a matter of deciding you are indeed going to take up your ideal career rather than just thinking wistfully about it. Express your decision in simple language. If, for example, your dream career is running your own outdoor adventure business specialising in white-water rafting, you might state your goal like this: "I'm going to run a white-water rafting business." Better still, adopt the language of someone already running such a business so that you think yourself into that role: "I'm running a white-water rafting business."

## *2. Check your beliefs*

Ask yourself, "What beliefs do I have that could prevent me from achieving this goal?" or, "What fears do I need to overcome to be able to run this business successfully?" List everything that comes to mind, e.g. "I won't be good enough at running a business", "I'll never attract enough customers", "I don't have what it takes."

## 3. Create new beliefs

Think up empowering alternatives to the beliefs identified in step 2. They will state the opposite of those beliefs, and express what you want to be true, e.g.:

| Disempowering beliefs | Empowering alternatives |
|---|---|
| I won't be good enough at running a business | I'm more than good enough at running a business and I learn more each day |
| I'll never attract enough customers | I can easily attract all the customers I need |
| I don't have what it takes | I'm made of the right stuff to succeed in this business |

## 4. Set some learning goals

If some of the fears identified at step 2 concern a real (rather than imagined) lack of knowledge or experience, you will need to decide how to address the deficiency. You may require business, marketing or sales skills, or perhaps you need greater proficiency with computers. It might be that you have to learn to communicate more effectively, or to improve your knowledge of the latest technical developments in your chosen field. Extra education can help you reach your goals, and fortunately there is no shortage of sources. Check out courses available at your local centres of education. There are many evening or part-time courses on offer, which are less demanding on time and finances than full-time education. Think, too, what you might do without resorting to formal learning, in the way of reading or talking to people with relevant knowledge and experience.

## 5. Create supercharged beliefs

Look five years into the future. You have been running your business for that time, perhaps expanded and developed it. You are one of the top operators, satisfying adventure seekers from all over the world. Someone is interviewing you to find out how you have become such a success. Imagine the questions they ask, and how you reply. Once they've covered the basics, such as, "How long have you been running this business?" and "How many customers do you have each season?", they get down to the interesting stuff: "What gave you the idea?", "How did you get started?", "Wasn't that a big risk?" (Answer: "Sure, but..." or "For some, perhaps, but..."), "What do you think you have that has enabled you to be such a success?", "How come you've achieved so much so quickly and confidently?" These questions are intended to get you to throw light on your attitude and key beliefs, your motivation and determination. Don't disappoint! Tell them all about your vision and how you have made it reality.

Use this process to formulate the beliefs necessary to reach all your goals. When your beliefs are in alignment with what you want to achieve, your progress will be smooth and swift. By asking yourself what beliefs you have that could sabotage your efforts, you can weed them out and replace them with alternatives that will have you rocketing towards your ideals.

# 16

## *Defining yourself*

W HAT kind of person do you need to be to actually live the awesome life you have designed for yourself? Do you need to change how you think about yourself? Is your current perception of who you are in alignment with who you want to be, or is it based on the past? You have defined what you want; now it's time to define yourself. When you do this in terms of your vision of who you want to become, that is who you *will* become. By defining yourself you can stop searching and start being.

How you define yourself will influence the things you do. To change your behaviour, simply change the way you define yourself. If the definition you have of yourself includes being confident, you will behave confidently. You will demonstrate the qualities you consistently attribute to yourself. If you think of yourself as a passionate person, you will become a passionate person. If you describe yourself as excited about life, that is how you will behave. Disempowering habits can be changed by redefining yourself. If you are a smoker, consistently describing yourself as a non-smoker will help you give up. Decisions are based on self-image. I've watched people go from one personal-development seminar to another, spending large sums of money, in a quest to find a definition of who they are. Most are waiting for someone to give them permission to be someone or something. Ultimately it is up to you to define who you are.

# Create a personal profile

What is your ideal experience of yourself? What qualities do you want to attribute to yourself? The following is a list of statement openers you can use to create a personal profile (with example "answers" to start you off). When you have completed them, see if you can think of any others. Again, writing will force you to be specific.

- I experience myself as... (confident/self-directed/relaxed...)
- A priority for me is... (learning to expand daily my capacity to love/to understand others/to share my sense of humour...)
- I'm committed to... (knowing the deepest part of myself/developing an ever more rewarding relationship with my partner...)
- I'm passionate about... (the beauty of nature/playing the piano/fine wine...)
- I enjoy the challenge of... (completing a task/maintaining my fitness/mastering a new computer program...)
- I love to share... (conversation/laughter/my enthusiasm for sport/music/movies...)
- It's important to me to... (have people around me who have interesting ideas to share/like me for who I am/share my concern for the environment...)
- I get immense pleasure from... (listening to music/tramping and camping/learning more about myself...)
- I'm highly skilled at... (communicating/being a host/making others feel at ease...)
- I get excited about... (all the possibilities in my life/the potential I have/being alive...)
- I'm the type of person who... (always sees the best in people/tends to see the funny side of things/believes in a pragmatic approach...)
- I'm committed to daily improving... (my ability to communicate/my attitude to life/the quality of my relationships...)
- My vision is one of... (perfect happiness for everyone/a

world living in harmony/all people fulfilling their potential...)
- I'm a confident... (guitarist/sailor/speaker...)
- I express my creativity by... (writing/singing/cooking...)
- I'm an example of... (someone who goes for it in life/ someone who is willing to take chances...)
- My values reflect... (my commitment to tolerance and goodwill/my desire to master my emotions/finances/career...)
- The feelings I enjoy experiencing consistently are... (love for my partner/the excitement of trying new things/satisfaction from a job well done...)

Read through your personal profile every day to align yourself with it. Your feelings, decisions and actions will all be influenced by it. Once it is implanted in your mind, you will become the "you" that you have defined.

As you grow and change and become aware of ever more possibilities in life, you will want to update your self-definition. Just as past conditioning is not cast in stone and can therefore be changed, neither is your personal profile.

## *Define your career profile*

One of the ways in which we are most commonly defined by society at large is in terms of the work we do. One of the first things people tend to ask each other on introduction is, "What do you do?" A person's job provides a convenient label, an initial handle on where they fit into the general scheme of things. As a rule we all play along with this, not only asking others about their occupations but offering in return information about our own and hence defining ourselves for their benefit. Because of the significance we attach to our occupations, and the necessity of earning a living in a consumer society, this aspect of self-definition is worthy of special attention.

If you *define* yourself as an artist, say, your behaviour will tend to include actions and activities associated with *being* an artist. If you define yourself as an entrepreneur, your behaviour will include seeking out business opportunities.

167

You can define yourself most meaningfully by referring to the values your work exemplifies, or the functions you perform. For instance, if you are a mother, you can be described as a provider of nourishment, a chief, an inspirer, a teacher, a nurse and health promoter, a coach, a financial manager, an events organiser, a chauffeur, a friend, a confidante, an entertainer, a valet and a seamstress — to name but a few aspects of this demanding vocation.

If you want to change careers yet continue to describe yourself the way you have always done, effecting a change will be difficult. A number of years ago, when I wanted to make the break from house decorating to a career that encompassed my passion for self-awareness, I found I was struggling. Although I had redefined what I wanted, I hadn't redefined myself. My self-image was that of a decorator, yet I was leading workshops and teaching rebirthing. My mind was screaming, "What do you think you're doing? You should be out there decorating?" Because what I was doing was at odds with my old but surviving image of who I was, I was experiencing anxiety. My new behaviour didn't fit my old image. Once I redefined myself as a workshop organiser, facilitator and rebirther, my mind changed tack completely. I now felt anxiety at the thought of decorating! And the twin drives to avoid pain and pursue pleasure motivated me not to decorate again and to be true to my new self-image. Both before and after redefining myself, I experienced anxiety when I acted, or even thought about acting, in a way that opposed my self-image. *If your behaviour doesn't match your perception of who you are, you will experience anxiety.* This is a classic example of how cognitive dissonance can influence your behaviour. Your behaviour will always be congruent with the way you perceive yourself.

■ Man's main task is to give birth to himself

Erich Fromm

Whatever you want to be, define yourself as such and you will find yourself compelled to become it. The way you define yourself will also influence the way you perceive the world around you. You will notice things that are relevant to who you have become. When I first started describing myself as a writer, I was amazed at all the valuable resources I came across. I found helpful books on friends' bookshelves and articles about successful writers in magazines and newspapers. When you remake yourself, opportunities you didn't notice before become apparent.

Draw up a career profile based on your career ideals. What qualities would define you in your career? How would you portray what you do? Someone in my line of business might say they were a catalyst for personal change, a contributor of value, a teacher of high self-esteem and a breathing coach. Write your own career profile now:

- I'm a creator of...
- I teach...
- I'm a catalyst for...
- I'm a contributor of...
- I'm a producer of...
- I'm a promoter of...

When you have done this, compose one powerful "I am..." statement that sums up your career. Remember, however you describe what you do, that is what you will move towards. It's a good idea to highlight in your statement a few of the qualities to which you attach particular importance. For instance, you can emphasise confidence by stating, "I'm a confident...", or attention to detail by stating, "I'm a meticulous..." You can be specific by saying, "I'm a... specialising in..." One of the first career statements I formulated for myself was, "I'm a relaxed, confident, and internationally known and supported seminar leader and author." Bear in mind that your statement needs to be easy to remember, so keep it simple.

What sort of effect do you think consistent repetition to yourself of your career statement will have had after, say, a year? Do you think you'll be moving in that direction? You can guarantee it. And after ten years? You'll be living it, well and truly. The key is to start now. Apart from not defining what they want in the first place, the main reason most people don't achieve their dreams is that they don't think they're worth the time and effort it would take. In other words, they give up before they've even started. Nothing changes until you change. All change happens on the inside first. If you want to experience something different next month, and in two years' time, you must start the process of change *now*. One little change now can make a huge difference to where you find yourself in the future. Simple actions have a profound effect.

By reviewing your values and ideals, visualising your future, and defining your personal and career profiles, you are building the life you desire and taking control of your destiny. You now know what you want; the next step is to learn how to keep yourself on track and heading in the right direction by using feedback.

# 17

## *Feedback: your personal guidance system*

ONCE you have prepared for and embarked upon the voyage to your desired future, you need a guidance system that can keep you on course. We all have immediate access to the personal guidance system of feedback. Your life experiences will tell you what adjustments you need to make to reach your destination. Every experience you have, no matter how unrelated it may seem to your actions, tells you something about yourself. To gain a clear understanding of feedback and how it works, it is useful to turn for a moment to a consideration of what scientists call systems theory.

We live in an interactive universe. On subtle and not so subtle levels we are all connected. This is the basis of systems theory. Instead of defining an individual as a separate entity, systems theory considers the individual as a part of a unified, purposeful system that is composed of interrelated parts. What takes place in one part of the system influences what happens in other parts, which, in turn, affects what happens in yet others — and so on.

Your mind and body comprise a system in which information is being continuously transmitted backwards and forwards between all the constituent parts. Each of us is a part of our family, all the members of which interact in a million different ways. The family system is in turn a part of the cultural system. The Western culture is part of an even bigger system made up of all the world's cultures, which share information and bear upon each other in various ways.

One could continue indefinitely. On a personal level, we each process information that we receive from our environment. From this information we form conclusions, expectations and beliefs which shape how we perceive and respond to the world around us. Our mental state and the behaviour it motivates shape our environment, producing circumstances we then experience. What we experience equals yet more information, which we process and act upon — and so it continues. This information is our feedback. Thus systems theory provides a framework within which we can plan actions and anticipate both their immediate and long-term consequences. It also allows us to determine the cause of what we experience, and hence to modify that cause so we obtain a different outcome.

Every day we are made increasingly, and painfully, aware of how interconnected the natural environment is with human activities. A tropical rainforest is a good example of a system. Huge numbers of animals and plants live together in ecological balance, dependent on each other for their survival. We assume such rich proliferation must be supported by incredibly fertile soil, yet all the nutrients necessary for the forest's luxuriant growth are produced by a thin layer of rotting vegetation on the forest floor. Once the trees are removed, so is the source of much of the goodness that allowed their growth.

Rainforests are a part of, and therefore influence, an even greater system — the planet. When we destroy rainforests, the climate is affected. When we pump toxic waste into the air, it forms acid rain and the health of our forests and lakes is affected. If we clear bush off the hills, the land erodes. Within a system every action creates a reaction, or result, in another part of the system — in other words, feedback. This is just as much the case on a personal level as on an environmental level.

A systems approach provides a way of perceiving oneself as an integral part of a greater whole. There is a direct relationship between someone's thinking and behaviour, and what takes place in their body and in their environment. We are well aware that we respond to our environment — so much is evident from our childhood conditioning. We are often not so aware that our environment responds to us. Every thought we entertain and every action we take produces some form of response, the feedback in terms of which we can describe the experiences we have in life. Everything is feedback, and the use of feedback is the key to controlling and maintaining continuous movement in our desired direction of progress. We often unconsciously use the information feedback gives us to reinforce what we already believe to be true; but rather than using it to prop up or justify old, disempowering beliefs, we can use it to change, grow and become more self-aware. This is the key distinction of the conscious use of feedback. By assessing feedback we can continually modify our beliefs and behaviour until our experience is exactly what we want it to be. Our beliefs and behaviour are always the cause of the feedback we receive.

We receive *internal* feedback in the form of responses to our environment and other people, intuitive thoughts, feelings and emotions. If we feel unhappy, on top of the world or fearful, those feelings are feedback. If we hate our job, the sense of dissatisfaction is feedback. If we become ill, the particular symptoms we experience are feedback. *External* feedback, on the other hand, is everything that happens to us or around us. This includes how people respond to us; for example, others may be helpful, loving or angry toward us — all feedback. If we crash our car, that is feedback. How much money we have, what possessions we own and the events that take place in our lives are all feedback.

For a moment, consider life as a game and your experience of the game as feedback. By analysing your feedback you discover where on the playing board you are, and can thus decide what your next move will be to get to where you want to go. Here are some simple rules by which to play:

**1.** *You must accept responsibility for the results you obtain.* It might be tempting to claim that you aren't responsible for certain things in your life, but, although your family, the government, the economy, other people and circumstances

173

inevitably influence you in various ways, to use your life experiences as feedback you must accept your role as creator.

**2.** *Tell yourself the truth about your results.* Honesty about your experience is essential if you are to make use of feedback to grow. This includes acknowledging the truth about your feelings. If you deny feelings of anger, sadness and helplessness, you won't be able to resolve them.

**3.** *Suspend blame and judgement.* It is very common for people, once they realise that thoughts create reality, to shift from blaming others for their circumstances to blaming themselves. Blaming yourself and blaming others are equally unhelpful. Simply recognise that, to produce the results you want, you need to change your approach. Life presents you with many opportunities for growth and healing. Be grateful for everything with which you are dissatisfied — it is all feedback which you can use to get to know your true self.

## Use feedback to transform your life

### 1. Know your desired outcome

What is your goal? What do you want to achieve? Create a clear description of what it is you want to experience.

### 2. Design your strategy

You know the outcome you want; now design a strategy that you think will produce that outcome. What actions are most likely to take you where you want to go? What new beliefs do you need to adopt in order to create what you want?

### 3. Take action

This is the doing part. Put your strategy to work and get some results. The sooner you take action, the sooner you will be provided with feedback.

## 4. *Assess your feedback*

Once you have taken action, you will receive feedback. Compare it with your desired outcome. Are they the same? If not, what changes do you need to make to your strategy to achieve what you want? This is an opportunity to refine your approach. Do your beliefs or behaviour need adjusting? Keep honing your strategy until it delivers the results you are after.

When you are analysing feedback, be as specific as possible. For instance, if your goal is to change how you feel and you describe your feeling as "uncomfortable", you have very little to go on. If, on the other hand, you define your feeling as "anxiety about not having enough money and being on a low income", you have something concrete with which to work. You can set a goal that will increase your income, and design a strategy that includes both the adoption of a new set of beliefs about money and actions that will start to move you in the direction of your goal. The more accurately you describe the experience you are dissatisfied with, the better your chances of designing an effective strategy. Ask yourself specific questions such as, "What response am I getting?", "How would I describe this problem?", "What belief do I have that could be responsible for this situation?" and "What have I been thinking or doing that has created this?" Your feelings can give you valuable clues as to what your beliefs are. Feeling rejected can indicate the belief "People reject me" or "I'm not wanted." Feeling ripped off could indicate the belief "I can't trust people." Ask yourself, "How do I feel about this experience?" Pinpoint the specific beliefs and behaviour that need to be changed.

Once you have assessed your feedback go back to step 1 and check your desired outcome. If your feedback and outcome match up, you know your strategy for change is working.

When using the above steps, it might be helpful to think of them as forming a continuous process or *feedback loop*. You continue round and round the loop until you achieve your desired outcome. There are two points at which you can start on this loop. The first is obvious — step 1.

Let's say you wish to experience more fun in your relationship with your partner. This is your desired outcome. Having identified this, you need to design a strategy to achieve it (step 2); you might, for instance, schedule a number of fun events you know you will both enjoy. Perhaps you are also aware that you tend to be rather serious and find it hard to relax, which limits the fun you are capable of experiencing. Your strategy could therefore also include adopting new beliefs in keeping with a lighter attitude to life and a more relaxed disposition. Then you take action (step 3) — that is, you do the fun things you've scheduled, you work at changing your beliefs and you practise relaxing. You might continue in this way for, say, a month, at which stage you assess your feedback (step 4). You contemplate the changes that have taken place in your relationship and compare them with your desired goal. Are you experiencing more fun? Have you developed a lighter attitude? Are you relaxing more? What other changes do you notice? Define exactly what you are experiencing.

There are several outcomes you could experience at this point. One is you have reached your goal and are quite satisfied. All that remains is to ensure you keep up the momentum and don't slip back into the old ways. The second is you have reached your goal but now realise that fun is only one aspect of your relationship that needed a boost. You might decide to restate your goal, taking your other requirements, such as increased excitement, love and support, into consideration. In this case, you will have to design a fresh strategy and go round the feedback loop again. Thirdly, you may not have succeeded in making any change at all. Assuming you did take the action you planned but it hasn't produced the results you are after, you will have to design a new strategy that you think will be more effective.

Sometimes you will be unsure exactly what you do want but have a very good idea of what you don't want because it is already happening and causing you concern. In such a case you start on the feedback loop at the second point of entry, step 4, by first assessing your feedback, for that is precisely what the difficulty you are experiencing is — feedback. This is the option you will automatically take when there is something in your life you aren't satisfied with and you decide to do something about it. Perhaps you have a problem in your relationship. You haven't set a goal in this area to put things right, but it is obvious something has to change. By starting with the problem, you are starting at step 4. You need to assess the situation and clarify exactly what it is you are unhappy about. Then you can move on to step 1 and define what you want to experience instead, stating this as your goal, before devising a solution (step 2) and taking action (step 3) — and so on round the loop until you reach your desired outcome.

 *Peace cannot be kept by force. It can only be achieved by understanding*

Albert Einstein

## *Learning*

You can use feedback to bring your entire life into harmony with your highest aspirations, but don't always expect to get it right at the first attempt. Progress may be gradual; each time you go round the feedback loop you will learn something new and make fresh and finer distinctions, so you will reach your goal eventually. This progression, or learning curve, is sometimes steady; improvement is obvious and measurable at each completion of the loop, so throughout the whole process you can see your goal getting closer. When change happens in this way, it is enjoyable and encouraging. On other occasions, even though you're making consistently finer distinctions about how to bring about your desired outcome, it will seem as if you're getting nowhere; you keep "falling off the bike", your relationships continue to end in drama or you're still losing money. Then, just as your emotional frustration hits peak levels and you're about to give up, it happens — you have a realisation, the last missing piece falls into place — quite probably something that has been right in front of you the whole time — and whammo!, you create the change you want.

In whichever of these two ways change comes about, what we are doing is perfecting a strategy that creates the results we want. People succeed because they have found an effective strategy that produces the outcome they desire. They may not necessarily be aware of precisely what it is they are doing, but they know whatever it is works, and we can model the strategies of those who succeed in producing the results we are after. However, strategies are made up of beliefs and behaviour, and although we can "pinch" one we may be unaware of the significance of, or not fully understand, certain aspects of it, and these we have to figure out for ourselves as we apply it and repeatedly circumnavigate the feedback loop.

It may seem obvious to say that desired results may not be obtained at the first attempt, and that repeated effort, ever more focused and refined, is required. But the point is worth emphasising because of the temptation at a failed first — or at least early — attempt, to think of oneself as a failure and shy away from trying again. This is insane thinking, but to many people, making a mistake implies having done something wrong — yet mistakes are an integral part of the learning process. Mistakes and learning go hand in hand, so why do we call them mistakes? A mis-take isn't any such thing — it's a meant-take. To fear mistakes is to fear learning, growth and change.

Rather than being afraid of failing, what we are really afraid of is being *seen* to fail, and the disapproval and stigma this may bring. If there was no-one else on the planet to witness you trying and possibly not succeeding, would you fear failing? Probably not. The fear of making mistakes stems from low self-esteem.

There is no "wrong". In an evolving universe all events and circumstances have a function, even though we may judge them with our limited mind and vision as "bad" or "wrong". If we didn't create pollution, would we be learning about ecology and would we be realising the interdependence of all things? If, in order to appreciate the value of pure water, it becomes necessary for us to make it undrinkable, so be it. If there is no water to drink, its value will at last be appreciated. The same goes for air; we will most certainly appreciate clean air when it burns the throat to breathe. If we didn't experience pain, would we know and appreciate pleasure? If we didn't know fear, would we value love? If we didn't believe in separation, would we value oneness? Through the act of changing our mind about our experience, we discover our power. Out of crisis, stress and perturbation, our consciousness grows.

Everything that happens in your life is an opportunity for you to know a greater truth. Every moment is perfect in that it leads to the next. If you think about your life as evolving, you will see that whatever you are experiencing now plays an essential part in the creation of your future. Any point along the evolutionary path is necessary for progress to the next.

In a personal relationship you may experience a conflict that is the result of the beliefs and behaviour — the strategy — that you bring to it. If you consider the conflict a chance to create changes that will allow you to experience greater intimacy, the conflict can be considered perfect. Everything you experience is a part of you; therefore, look on it lovingly.

Focus your energy on creating the outcomes you want and take any mistakes in your stride. On the way to achieving your goals you may learn about many things that don't work and take many unnecessary steps. If you have high self-esteem, this won't bother you. You must learn to love and accept yourself, maintaining a sense of self-worth throughout the learning process. When you make a mistake, you have done something very right!

# 18

## Trust: the difference it makes

*T*RUST is a fundamental issue that has far-reaching implications. Self-trust has a powerful influence on one's ability to achieve one's goals. To know what you want isn't enough; you must also trust yourself to be able to do it, and that means having faith in the creative process of cause and effect. A lack of self-trust reduces self-discipline and may cause you to doubt your potential and creativity, as well as reducing your effectiveness in leadership roles. You can hardly expect others to trust you if you don't trust yourself. Have faith in your decisions and that what you want will come about.

An area in which trust plays a particularly important role is relationships. Where there is no trust, there is no basis for a relationship. If we don't trust someone, we are cautious and on guard, wary of giving too much of ourselves and always suspicious of attack or the possibility of manipulation or abuse. Without trust, honest communication becomes an impossibility.

A lack of trust creates mental and physical stress, making it very difficult to relax. To relax, we need to be assured we are safe, and a sense of safety cannot prevail unless trust is evident. So — is it other people who are the problem? Well, there are certainly plenty of people we wouldn't trust, and it's very easy to say, "I don't trust you." But when it comes down to it, *trust begins at home*, and the question isn't "Can I trust you?" as much as "Can I trust myself?" The belief "I don't trust myself" becomes, when projected, "I don't trust you", "I don't trust the government", "I don't trust the world", etc. It is the level of trust we have for ourselves that determines the extent to which we are capable of experiencing trust and safety with others.

In the same way that we project our lack of self-trust onto other people, we can project it onto the techniques, processes and systems we use, thereby lessening the likelihood that they will produce the results we are after. Next time your computer gives you a hard time or you have doubts about the technique you are using, check inside yourself. You may find your level of self-trust needs a boost.

Intuition is another area in which trust is important, as discussed earlier, and is a good place to start building self-trust and becoming aware of what it feels like both to trust and not to trust. Imagine asking someone you totally trust not to eat any of the chocolate cake you have just made until you get back. What does trusting them feel like? Now imagine asking someone you absolutely do not trust the same thing. What does that feel like? So often when someone or something disappoints us, the doubts are there right from the start. We have a feeling or sense that something is off. We want to say no, but we say yes, or vice versa. Intuitively we know the right choice to make. At first, trusting your intuition can be a bit scary, but you will soon learn that doing so always leads you in the right direction.

Run a check on your level of self-trust by reading these affirmations and taking enough time to note your response to each one:

- I trust myself
- I trust life
- I trust my feelings
- I trust my intuition
- I trust myself financially
- I trust my sexuality
- I trust my body
- I trust my ability to heal myself
- I trust that I will do what I say I will do

- I trust my ability to get what I want
- I trust myself in the presence of others
- I trust that I am safe
- I trust my judgement and decisions
- I trust that there is enough love for me
- I trust that there is enough money for me
- I trust that my needs will always be taken care of
- I trust that people will love and support me
- I trust my creative power
- I trust that I can and will achieve my goals
- I trust that my life is evolving perfectly
- I trust myself to be honest

## *The key to feeling safe*

Questioning and changing your beliefs will take courage and commitment, but this price is worth paying for the greater freedom and happiness it will buy. An effective way of building self-trust is to develop the discipline of following through with the things you say you are going to do. Start with little things. If you say you are going to get out of bed at 6.00 a.m., do it. When you do, you will quickly develop that little extra self-trust and your self-esteem will rise accordingly. The more you trust yourself and life, the more you will radiate an energy of trust. People will feel safe in your presence and you will attract other trusting people into your sphere. You will be able to relax and feel safe in the world, and it will indeed start to feel that the universe is a secure, supportive and loving place to be and that your life is evolving perfectly. Where there is trust, there is safety. In the presence of safety, love flows and we can open up to a deeper experience of ourselves. It is always safe to relax, let go and trust.

# 19

## *Maintaining happiness*

O UR happiness isn't dependent on the things we have or achieve in our lives. If we base our happiness on these things, we will continually be frustrated. Why? Because we reach an *adaptation level*. This is a level of success or achievement to which we become accustomed. Whereas actually attaining a certain level of success may make us feel happy, later, once we have grown accustomed to our achievement, the happiness wanes and we are compelled to set new goals and expectations in order to experience the feeling afresh. This can become a continuous process of entrapment. We momentarily experience happiness, it passes, and we have to search for it again.

 What we are today comes from our thoughts of yesterday, and our present thoughts build our life of tomorrow: Our life is the creation of our mind

The Buddha

We can be so demanding of life, by wanting more and more and never being satisfied, that it never measures up. This sort of demanding is an expression of a compensatory need. We secretly believe we aren't good enough, and project this belief onto our achievements, our possessions, our partner and our job. We then try continuously to make our life "good enough". As Mick Jagger expresses it in one of his songs, "We make lots of money and we just want more." People climb the corporate ladder thinking that happiness awaits them at the top. Athletes compete to be the best in the world thinking that will bring them happiness. We climb the "have it all" scale and find happiness persistently elusive. We say, "I'll be happy when I've got my new car, a good income or find the right partner." How many times have you said, "I'll be happy when I get..." and as soon as you got it, without even acknowledging your achievement, you were aiming for the next thing you believed you needed to ensure happiness?

Alfie Kohn states in his book *No Contest*: "The discovery, ultimately, that 'making it' is often a hollow gain is one of the most traumatic events that a successful competitor can experience."* The sentiment this expresses holds equally true when applied to other areas in which people strive.

Demanding a lot out of life in an attempt to feel okay about oneself is very different from demanding a lot out of life because of a desire to explore, express and expand one's aliveness. Setting high standards and goals to support growth is quite different from doing so to prove oneself better than others.

True happiness is dependent on personal beliefs and attitudes. Our beliefs are the ultimate determiners of whether we will be happy or not. Adopt beliefs such as, "Everything I experience gives me happiness and joy", "Every breath I take gives me a feeling of happiness", "I'm happy to be alive" and "I'm happy with everything I have", and you will be happy — permanently. When you accept happiness as yours, you will have it always. Here are some simple and effective keys to creating and maintaining happiness.

## 1. Be grateful for everything you have

Happiness starts with being grateful for everything you have and are currently experiencing. This includes appreciating

*No Contest: The case against competition*, Houghton Mifflin, Boston, 1986

being alive in the first place. Find reasons to be grateful. Gratitude is an affirmation of happiness.

## 2. You already have everything you need to be happy

Right at this moment all your needs are being met. You may not have all the money, possessions or even love you would like, but you nevertheless already have everything you need to be happy. When you search for happiness outside of yourself, you presuppose that you don't have it, and as long as you continue to search outside, it will remain hidden. Don't put happiness off until you have reached your goals. You can be happy now, independent of achievement or situation.

## 3. Follow your true self

To be happy you need an experience of aliveness, and to have that you need to follow your true self. By doing so and experiencing the happiness it brings, you will set an example so others may do the same. Your happiness will expand when you share it; the more you share with others, the more you will experience yourself. To teach others, one has to focus on the subject being taught, and that which is focused on expands. Magnify your experience of happiness by following your true self.

## 4. Behave as if you are happy

Have you ever noticed the effect smiling has on your thinking and how you feel? When we smile, we feel good. You may have developed habitual facial expressions of anger, disappointment, sadness, fear, etc., such that when you unconsciously put on one of these faces you become disempowered. If you smile and look up slightly, you won't be able to remain disempowered. Smiling is a powerful tool for changing the way you feel. The tension that smiling creates in your facial muscles will send the message to your brain that you are in a happy state. You can change your emotional state instantly by changing the way you hold your face. Mastering the ability to take on empowering facial expressions, simple as it may sound, can transform your life.

Imagine you are looking up at a snow-covered mountain range towering above the clouds. The sun is just rising, casting a bright orange glow. You can feel the freshness of the early morning air; you can hear the morning birdsong. Immerse yourself fully in the surroundings. Feel the wonder and awe this scene inspires. Let your face take on the full emotion of the experience. While you are in this state, take note of how you are holding your face. Adopting the same facial expression in the future will allow you to re-create the same emotional state any time you wish. You can use this technique to experience virtually any emotional state you choose. Use your imagination to put yourself in the state you want, remember the details of the facial expression it produces, and duplicate it. You can develop expressions for feelings of wonder, discovery, inspiration, intrigue, fascination, curiosity, outrageousness, confidence, determination and amazement, to name but a few. The key to controlling your emotional states is to consistently reinforce the physiological patterns that give you the emotions you want. In other words, *if you want to be happy, express happiness!*

## 5. *The winner's smile*

One of the most disempowering emotions many people experience is that of feeling like a loser, that things just aren't working out. You can combat this by developing a "winner's smile". Model the expression of athletes as they experience the thrill and excitement of winning; there are plenty of examples on TV or in sports magazines and books. It is a total ear-to-ear smile, and might therefore use some muscles you haven't exercised much before! Use consistent repetition to make the winner's smile a part of your physiology that you can call on whenever you need a boost or want to get into an empowered state to take effective action. By using the smile, you will send a powerful message to your brain that says, "I'm a winner!"

# 20

## Your future: what's it to be?

*T*HE question has been posed throughout this book, what do you really want? It is time to ask it once again, in the hope that you will continue to ask it of yourself. A person's true self represents a state of love. *A Course in Miracles* says, "Teach love to have love."* The same principle can be applied to anything you desire. The purpose of teaching is to focus the student's mind on what he or she wishes to learn. We all teach all of the time; the question is, what are we teaching? We teach whatever we believe. By applying the law of cause and effect, you can choose to create a life that is unique to you. By following your own intuitive, internal guidance, you will teach others to do the same.

When we have a community of individuals who freely express themselves in their own unique, creative way, we shall have a community that is thriving. Imagine if every individual on the planet felt he or she had something of value to give and the courage to give it. Consider the sheer energy that would create. Imagine the momentum it would build. Think of the consequences for this or any other country's value as a nation, its wealth and everyone's standard of living. Imagine the kind of world we would have. Might it not be one in which people would be more effective in making the changes necessary to overcome the many overwhelming problems

* *A Course in Miracles*, Routledge & Kegan Paul, New York, 1975, and Arkana, London, 1985

currently facing mankind, problems such as poverty, hunger, interethnic conflict and environmental destruction? Only when we consciously think of and act for the highest evolutionary good of all will we reach the level of maturity and responsibility at which we can operate as one living organism, of which each of us makes up a small but vital part. As the individual evolves, so does the whole; as the whole evolves, so does the individual. We are inseparable.

> The earth is a paradise, the only one we will ever know — We will realise it the moment we open our eyes. We don't have to make it a paradise — it is one. We have only to make ourselves fit to inhabit it
>
> Henry Miller

Change starts with individuals — with you and me. It starts with changing the quality of our thoughts, our feelings and our actions. The world needs men and women who have the courage to express themselves, to create a society which encourages others to do likewise and supports people in learning about who they are and how to realise their full potential. It needs systems that allow people to grow and expand, not systems that seek to mould and restrict.

If no-one speaks up and starts the process of change, what will happen? Are we going to let our planet go down the gurgler through apathy or for fear of making a stand? Are we going to continue to bring up children who perpetuate beliefs and behaviour detrimental to the future of all humankind? You can make a difference now by changing your own beliefs, aiming for new ways of being, and developing strategies for achieving the results you desire. We all want to make changes in our lives — in our relationships, finances, health or some other area. Making change is a challenge, but it is one to which we are all equal.

There is a principle operating in the universe that would have us succeed. You can call it God, the Great Spirit, energy or simply life. Whatever you name it, this principle seems to intend us to be all we can be. What greater satisfaction than to use your life to guide yourself to an ever fuller realisation of who you are? Choose to have a positive impact on yourself, your family, your friends and the environment. Empower yourself now. Question the past, live in the present and build an inspiring future. Above all — follow your true self.

# Further reading

*A Course in Miracles*, Routledge & Kegan Paul, New York, 1975, and Arkana, London, 1985

Allen, James, *As a Man Thinketh*, Grosset & Dunlop, New York, 1980

Buckminster Fuller, R., *Critical Path*, St Martin's Press, New York, 1981

Covey, Stephen R., *Principle-Centred Leadership*, Simon & Schuster, New York, 1991

Goldberg, Natalie, *Wild Mind: Living the writer's life*, Rider, London, 1991

Horney, Karen, *Neurosis and Human Growth: The struggle towards self-realisation*, Routledge & Kegan Paul, London, 1951

Kohn, Alfie, *No Contest: The case against competition*, Houghton Mifflin, Boston, 1986

Leonard, Jim, and Laut, Phil, *Rebirthing: The science of enjoying all of your life*, Trinity Publications, Hollywood, Cal., 1985

Maslow, Abraham, *Toward a Psychology of Being*, Van Nostrand Reinhold, New York, 1968

Miller, Alice, *For Your Own Good: Hidden cruelty in child-rearing and the roots of violence*, Farrar Straus Giroux, New York, 1988

Monte, Christopher F., *Beneath the Mask: An introduction to theories of personality*, Holt, Rinehart & Winston, 1987

Ray, Sondra, and Mandel, Bob, *Birth and Relationships: How your birth affects your relationships*, Celestial Arts, Berkeley, Cal., 1987

Roddick, Anita, *Body and Soul*, Vermillion, London, 1992

Toffler, Alvin, *The Third Wave: The revolution that will change our lives*, Collins, 1980

# Index